About Island Press

Since 1984, the nonprofit Island Press has been stimulating, shaping, and communicating the ideas that are essential for solving environmental problems worldwide. With more than 800 titles in print and some 40 new releases each year, we are the nation's leading publisher on environmental issues. We identify innovative thinkers and emerging trends in the environmental field. We work with world-renowned experts and authors to develop cross-disciplinary solutions to environmental challenges.

Island Press designs and implements coordinated book publication campaigns in order to communicate our critical messages in print, in person, and online using the latest technologies, programs, and the media. Our goal: to reach targeted audiences—scientists, policymakers, environmental advocates, the media, and concerned citizens—who can and will take action to protect the plants and animals that enrich our world, the ecosystems we need to survive, the water we drink, and the air we breathe.

Island Press gratefully acknowledges the support of its work by the Agua Fund, Inc., The Margaret A. Cargill Foundation, Betsy and Jesse Fink Foundation, The William and Flora Hewlett Foundation, The Kresge Foundation, The Forrest and Frances Lattner Foundation, The Andrew W. Mellon Foundation, The Curtis and Edith Munson Foundation, The Overbrook Foundation, The David and Lucile Packard Foundation, The Summit Foundation, Trust for Architectural Easements, The Winslow Foundation, and other generous donors.

The opinions expressed in this book are those of the author(s) and do not necessarily reflect the views of our donors.

Community Character

Community Character

Principles for Design and Planning

◆

Lane H. Kendig

with

Bret C. Keast

Washington | Covelo | London

Library of Congress Cataloging-in-Publication Data

Kendig, Lane.
 Community character : principles for design and planning / Lane H. Kendig with Bret C. Keast.
     p. cm.
Includes bibliographical references and index.
ISBN-13: 978-1-59726-695-6 (cloth : alk. paper)
ISBN-10: 1-59726-695-7 (cloth : alk. paper)
ISBN-13: 978-1-59726-696-3 (pbk. : alk. paper)
ISBN-10: 1-59726-696-5 (pbk. : alk. paper)
1. Community development—Planning. 2. Rural development—Planning. I. Keast, Bret C. II. Title.
HN49.C6K457 2010
307.1′2—dc22   2009050777

Printed using Dante

Text design by Karen Wenk
Typesetting by Karen Wenk

Printed on recycled, acid-free paper

Manufactured in the United States of America
10 9 8 7 6 5 4 3 2 1

To my wife,
Elaine Van S. Carmichael

Contents

Acknowledgments   xi

Introduction: Why Should We Care About Community Character?   1

1 The Designer's Lexicon   9

2 Community State, Context, and Scale   37

3 Community Character Classes and Types   67

4 Community and Regional Forms   111

5 Community Character Measurement   139

6 Conclusion   167

Notes   173
Index   179

Acknowledgments

I am indebted first to Franklin C. Wood, executive director of the Bucks County Planning Commission (Pennsylvania), where I was first employed as a planner. Franklin's approach to managing staff was to support planners pursuing new ideas rather that to limit them, as is the case in most agencies. His support allowed me to develop Performance Zoning, with its character-based rather than density-based districts. Second is Fred Bosselman, who in a speech at an American Planning Association conference in the late 1970s argued that community character was a powerful but unused planning tool. Fred's speech led me to question what elements make up different community characters, and how that character is measured. As the Lake County (Illinois) planning director, I proposed that Performance Zoning using character districts be used. A new comprehensive plan for Lake County was put in development (the 1982 Framework Plan), and it became the first comprehensive conception of a community-character-based system of planning. The following year Lane Kendig inc. (now Kendig Keast Collaborative) was formed, and in the next few years all the basic elements of character as presented here were developed. The character system has been used in all the firm's planning and zoning work throughout the country (which includes counties as well as small and large cities and site plans for a wide range of uses). This has served to test the validity of and further refine the material presented herein.

For the production of this book, I would first like to thank Elaine Carmichael for her review and research on the economic elements of community character. Many employees at Kendig Keast Collaborative have worked on plans and ordinances using community character, and I appreciate their effort and support. A number of the staff have assisted with some of the graphics and photos in the book—particularly Bret C. Keast (figure 2-11), Jon Arndt (figures 1-45, 1-46, 3-25, 3-38b), Elizabeth Austin (figures 5-4, 5-7, 5-8, 5-9, 5-10), Jon Grosshans (for reformatting and reference work), and Todd Messenger (figures 1-36, 1-37, 1-41, 1-42)—and their support has been important to the timely delivery of graphics. All the other photographs and drawings in the book are by the author. Sharon McConnell has provided assistance with editing and other work for many years. Last but not least, I would like to thank my editors, Heather Boyer, Courtney Lix, and Sharis Simonian for helping me through the process and responding to my needs.

Lane Kendig

Why Should We Care About Community Character?

Character is often used to describe the elements of a community that make it unique, memorable, livable, and inviting. These elements can be hard to define. An often-heard example is a desire to "preserve small town character." This isn't just a motherhood-and-apple-pie vision, but can be defined or measured using community character tools. In this book I introduce those tools—a community character system for describing the physical form of communities and resulting lifestyle, residential, work, and retail opportunities. It provides a systematic approach to converting vague visions or goals of citizens and officials to measurable elements that can be made into a plan.

The community character system has four major elements—state, scale, class and type of character, and community form—each of which provides the tools for planners to plan a development, neighborhood, or municipality. State and scale in particular are intended to make planners and citizens more aware of how their community functions and the consequences of planning or zoning decisions. Scale is powerfully linked to shopping, employment, and cultural opportunities. Those opportunities benefit known populations and service areas. Increasing scale results in changing work patterns and increased commercial, resulting in increased traffic volumes and congestion. The character types also relate to social and economic aspects of the community. Type involves three classes of character—urban, sub-urban, and rural—that are divided into eight types: urban core, urban, auto-urban, suburban, estate, countryside, agriculture, and natural. These focus on design elements that create the character types. The last major element—form—addresses three principal strategies for the design of settlements: compositional, group, and mega. Planning and architectural literature has primarily focused on the urban character type.

The number of elements composing character reflects the complexity of the built environment's interaction with the social and economic objectives and diverse desires of municipalities and citizens. Flexibility is essential. A planning approach that retains or enhances community character cannot be rigid; it must provide principles to be applied, rather than a template that merely dictates street width or how a building is placed on a lot.

WHY COMMUNITY CHARACTER?

Community character is a powerful tool that can incorporate architectural or environmental context to provide a community with a strong vision that carries through to zoning regulations. For example, in 1994 Teton County and the Town of Jackson, Wyoming, adopted a plan and zoning ordinance based on community character by using seven of the eight character types. The regulations contained a limitation on house size to keep new, large homes in scale with existing ranches and to limit the visual impact that new development would have on the area's scenic beauty. A person who illegally built a larger home unsuccessfully challenged the regulations in the courts. The following quotes from the Wyoming Supreme Court illustrate the power of character: "Teton County's choice of the word 'character' in conjunction with the words 'rural' and 'western' connotes something that is quite clear, especially given Teton County's documentation of the plan. . . . Indeed, preserving community character is at the very heart of zoning and planning legislation."[1]

Since New York City adopted zoning in 1916 and the U.S. Supreme Court upheld its legality in *Euclid v. Ambler Realty Co.* in 1926, the practice has been an important tool in protecting neighborhood character. Go to a zoning hearing today and you will hear citizens concerned that some proposed use will destroy the "character" of their neighborhood. This continued citizen concern means planners must do a better job of understanding and protecting character.

There are six primary reasons for understanding and using a community character system as a tool. First, protecting character was the primary rationale for zoning, which is the planner's primary tool for implementing plans.[2] Second, although character provided the rationale for zoning, plans and zoning were based largely on land use and density, neither of which measures the character or quality of development. Third, while there are eight types of character, the existing literature focuses almost exclusively on one of three urban types, providing no design guidance for the other seven types. Fourth, there has been a succession of architectural visions of the urban ideal that have failed, yet we are now seeing a new batch of architect-driven visions peddled as the universal template (see below). Fifth, while the design of communities is very important, there are social, economic, environmental, cultural, and other physical elements linked to character that must be understood if physical planning is to be realistic. Lastly, there must be a means to measure character so it is not just a concept that sounds nice but cannot be reliably converted to a design or regulation.

Over the last hundred years there has been a succession of architectural visions of the ideal form of communities. World-famous architects Le Corbusier and Frank Lloyd Wright held mutually exclusive views. Le Corbusier championed an urban community of stark, high- and medium-rise buildings, while Wright envisioned Broadacre City, a low-density community largely dependent on automobiles. The Le Corbusier model can be blamed to some degree for the soulless public housing disasters in American cities, and the Wright model can be blamed for inviting suburban sprawl. Paolo Soleri took a totally different approach by advocating that whole cities be created as a single building. While this extreme approach has never been realized, it has potential value at a smaller scale. The latest of these architecturally dominated approaches, the Transect,[3] is being promoted by New Urbanists as a universal template. The New Urbanist movement seeks a return to well-designed urban places, but the model advocated by some New Urbanists is nearly as rigid as the very zoning they decry.

The approaches of these architects, past and present, have value for individual projects, but their rigidity and template character make them unsuited for planning entire communities. These approaches attempt to fit people into the architect's vision. Planning for community character recognizes the full range of physical environments that people want or that function demands; it is a palette with many different components.

This approach identifies the critical elements and design principles of each character type and the unique characteristics of each community, in order to retain the character or guide the community over time to a new character.

Comprehensive plans for communities look at character, form, or land use as only one element of the overall vision. Social, cultural, economic, recreation, and transportation elements are equally important to the success of the plan, but are generally separated as topics from the physical form and character of the community. The community character system outlined here seeks to link the physical to social, economic, cultural, environmental, and other elements. It also recognizes that different characters represent differing lifestyle preferences.

Both comprehensive plans and zoning ordinances have been based on two quantifiable measures: density and land use. The focus on density is perhaps the more troubling of the two, because the average citizen erroneously believes that higher density threatens community character, which has resulted in much low-density, sprawling development. In reality this is not usually the case, as seen in figures 0-1a and 0-1b, where the lower-density example (0-1a) is viewed by most as having a less-desirable character than the higher-density example (0-1b). Density is not an accurate measure of character, as architects have long known. Evaluating the character or quality of a neighborhood and then determining the appropriate density would likely lead to more compact, livable communities.

Figure 0-1a. Density: one dwelling unit per acre, urban street cross section, open lawns. Chesterfield, Missouri.

Figure 0-1b. Density: three dwelling units per acre, rural street cross section, lawn maintained in native forest vegetation. New Seabury, Massachusetts.

Land use has similar problems. Planners and citizens developed a hierarchy of land uses, with single-family being higher or better, and industry being lower or less desirable. This encourages separating uses, rather than designing them to fit the neighborhood character. In figures 0-2a and 0-2b, two commercial land uses have very different qualities and character types. This illustrates that most uses can be designed to the desired character. In fact, it is possible for most residential, commercial, and office land uses to be designed for community character in all five of the urban and sub-urban character types.

Commercial areas with buildings built to the sidewalk line can be of either low or high quality. A lack of sign control, landscaping, and architectural design results in low-quality urban, as seen in figure 0-3a. Attention to the architecture, street trees, signage control, and pavement details results in high-quality urban, as seen in figure 0-3b. It is the details of design that determine quality, not the use or application of the build to the sidewalk template rule.

In reviewing the design literature, the vast majority addresses only one of the eight character types present today—urban. Most do not mention scale, state, or form. Community character covers the full range of communities, and provides for both their measurement as well as their design for livability. This approach will enable planners to plan for all types of communities in order to meet resident needs.

The vision statements in most plans use words like "rural," "small town," "suburban," or "urban" that are not well

Figure 0-2a. Urban commercial: built to sidewalk line, street parking, 95 percent impervious. Carmel, California.

Figure 0-2b. Estate commercial: built in wooded area with trees in parking lot, 20 percent impervious. New Seabury, Massachusetts.

Figure 0-3a. Poor design, inconsistent facades, no trees, large signs means poor quality. McAllen, Texas.

Figure 0-3b. High-quality design provides architecture, landscaping, and sign control. Carmel, California.

defined or are unrelated to the zoning. For example, the district created to preserve rural land uses frequently permits subdivision into one- to five-acre suburban lots, which replaces rural land uses with homes. Likewise, a community vision that calls for the preservation of small town character while proposing to double in population is suspect. By quantifying character, it becomes possible to evaluate the plan for consistency.

As planners, it is obvious that while the character elements are fixed, they are in a dynamic relationship. The balance—the share of the population living in each of the three classes—responds to changes in technology, economics, and social desires. For most of history, communities were of the smallest (population) scale—hamlets and villages. These were freestanding communities where most of the population lived and worked the surrounding land. The fact that they were freestanding, separated from others by farm fields, created a strong visual character of urban communities dotting the rural landscape. Most of these communities were considered urban, even though they were economically dependent on the surrounding agricultural lands. Urban describes the relationship of buildings, streets, and spaces, where buildings crowd the street, creating enclosed spaces.

The automobile and skyscraper created two new character types—auto-urban and urban core—that vastly altered the balance among the urban, sub-urban, and rural classes. These advances shifted populations from small areas (freestanding communities) growing food and fiber to metropolitan areas (composite communities). In the United States, sub-urban types evolved from a trivial share of the population to a major share. With the development of the automobile, urban gave way to auto-urban. As planners or policymakers, having a comprehensive understanding of community character—state, scale, type, and form—is critical if plans and zoning are to produce communities that are livable and sustainable.

CHALLENGES FOR THE FUTURE

Planning is facing new challenges, especially global warming and the energy crisis. Many American communities are sprawling forms that rely on energy-gobbling automobiles. There is active debate about how planning should address these problems. Will we have to shift to a more urban character to reduce the use of automobiles, or will more efficient cars and alternative fuels offset the energy and global greenhouse-gas-emission problems? The current balance has a predominance of Americans living in sub-urban communities. How will changing attitudes and strategies regarding energy and global warming alter the balance among types?

Community character does not dictate the balance, but it is important for planners to understand the drivers for different types in order to provide guidance on how to achieve the desired character in any type of community. The desired character must be formulated by how society and technology confront these problems. Community character provides the tools to plan for communities of all states, scales, types, and forms. All will continue to exist even if the balance is drastically changed.

There is little written about why and how to take a comprehensive approach to community character. This book and the subsequent volume, *A Guide to Planning for Community Character*, have been developed to fill this void. *Community Character* begins by providing the needed vocabulary for planners and designers to understand and address character. Later chapters address three major ways of thinking about or describing character—state and scale, character types, and community forms—and explain how to measure character.

Community Character does not seek to dictate choice or

provide a template. The market, technology, and individual desires interact to constrain or encourage choices. The community character system makes no judgment as to the desirability of a character type, state, scale, or form. They all exist, and a new one may evolve in response to technology. All represent valid choices; the effort is to provide the design principles for the desired character type.

Too often the concern for character has been thought of as aesthetics, which vary in the eye of the beholder. Community character is not about beauty, but about the linkage between how our communities are designed and how they function. Individuals will vary in their opinion of character types. Their decision about a character type to live in is also affected by social and economic constraints. The community character system is value-neutral; all the character types are presented with their accompanying social and economic conditions. All types have a segment of the population that values them because they meet their needs. We live in a very diverse society, and that diversity is good. All the types and scales are needed, and have both positive and negative aspects that should be understood. Having all the types actually is beneficial to a rich and diverse society.

The next book will provide a detailed explanation of how to apply community character in a comprehensive plan, with chapters on designing urban, sub-urban, and rural character types. It also makes recommendations to address the challenges of the twenty-first century.

CHAPTER **1**   *The Designer's Lexicon*

Planning for community character requires that architects, planners, urban designers, policymakers, and citizens clearly communicate their goals. Planners must then write plans and ordinances to enable those goals to be met. Unfortunately, many of these groups seem to speak different languages. There are a considerable number of terms used by architects and urban designers that are not commonly used by citizens, elected officials, and planners. Likewise, planners tend to use a number of terms typically found only in zoning ordinances.

To help facilitate the discussion about community character goals, this chapter introduces a design and planning lexicon. A great number of the urban design and architecture terms have been in the literature for decades. This is true of some of the planning and landscape terms as well. In developing community character for suburban and rural areas, I have developed additional terms over the past thirty years.

This chapter is organized by topical areas, so terms are grouped by their relation to one another rather than alphabetically. It begins with three terms that describe major classes of character, and then explores space, mass, and other elements of which they are made. Another set of terms addresses organizing buildings or spaces. The chapter concludes with landscape terms, which address the physical environment, along with planning and zoning terms.

There are a number of terms that describe aspects of communities and human settlements. Three descriptive ways of relating to space are discussed here—architectural, garden, and landscape—which connect to how the three classes of character (urban, sub-urban, and rural) are seen.

DESCRIPTIVE TERMS

Architectural Space

This describes outdoor space that is enclosed by man-made structures to house businesses or families (see figure 1-1). Buildings and their layout define architectural space. The design of the space itself is architectural. Spaces are paved and greenery is limited to small planters or tiny yards. In general, impervious surfaces, buildings, roads, plazas, and parking occupy nearly all the land in architectural spaces.

Figure 1-1. Architectural space: created by buildings. Stockholm, Sweden.

Garden-Like

The term "garden-like" refers to a space in which landscape elements provide a setting for the building (see discussion of negative space, below). The space is green and pervious rather than paved (see figure 1-2). Garden-like is intended to represent the presence of vegetative mass that is equal to or greater than the building mass, and whose height is generally greater than that of the buildings. Its green nature and softer shapes directly contrast with the hard-edged architectural environment.

Figure 1-2. Garden-like space: created by trees that shelter and surround buildings. McHenry County, Illinois.

Landscape

The term "landscape" is intended to evoke a natural or agricultural environment that extends to the horizon (see figure 1-3). A landscape requires that the built environment be in the background and trivial. Landscape planning follows the same rules as landscape painting in that buildings and communities are diminished to background elements or hidden from view. A landscape exists when one can see to the horizon in all directions without buildings breaking the horizon line (see the section on infinite space, below). Their other characteristic is that as people or cars move through them, landscapes seem to flow or expand as the horizon changes with movement.

Figure 1-3. Landscape: view across a field to the horizon. Chattahoochee Hill Country, Georgia.

Mass

Buildings, stands of vegetation, and landforms are all volumes that occupy and fill space; visually, they appear as solids. Whether they are truly solids (as is the case with a large boulder), hollow (as a structure containing rooms), or spongy (as a dense stand of vegetation with a visual shell of leaves) is immaterial. It is the visual characteristic that is important. Solids are visual elements that are shown on plans. They can also be walls that are two-dimensional, having little volume. Solids may contain human activity within them, may contain a space, or may serve only as a visual barrier. Mass can also be considered positive volume that occupies space visually.

Space

In planning communities, space means exterior space, open to the sky. Architects use this concept of space, but they also use the term to refer to interior spaces (rooms). Space may be pervasive, as it is at sea, where it is unlimited to the horizon. At the other end of the spectrum it can be a tightly contained void or area between surrounding walls or buildings. For this reason different types of space are defined.

Positive space (see figure 1-4) is exterior space enclosed by buildings or walls (basically an outdoor room). Positive space is sometimes referred to as centripetal[1]—that is, the space pulls or focuses activities inward. The degree of *enclosure* is very important for a positive space. Failure to provide enclosure weakens the space. Enclosure, which contains and focuses activity, is a key element in urban design and is a measurable concept (see the section on distance/height, or D/H, ratio, page 31). It is also appropriate, in most cases, to consider positive space as architectural space since it is inseparable from its surrounding buildings and their architecture.[2]

Negative space is space that surrounds a building, as in figure 1-5. The space is considered centrifugal—it radiates out from the building, and the building is buffered by the space. Instead of the building enclosing space, space surrounds and highlights the building. Negative spaces, as the term is used here,

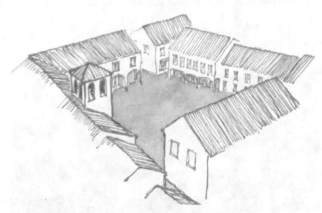

Figure 1-4. Positive space: buildings surround space.

Figure 1-5. Negative space: space surrounds building.

Figure 1-6. Borrowed space, from a house.

Figure 1-7. Infinite space: space extends to the horizon.

Figure 1-8. Hedge as a wall. South Island, New Zealand.

Figure 1-9. Trees as a screen partially block view of buildings.

may be highly designed, organized, and architectural.[3] As seen in figure 1-5, negative space is often surrounded by buildings, which focuses attention on the central building.

Borrowed space is a subset of negative space. Borrowed space "expands" the views from inside a building by creating either outdoor rooms or views of open space. It is not focusing attention on the building. The Japanese brought this concept to a high art form in designing small gardens to expand rooms (see figure 1-6). In planning, space is borrowed by the development, cluster, or community, not just a room in a house. Borrowed space may be a garden, a larger yard, or common open space. It can also be temporary, such as vacant land adjoining a development that can later be developed, thereby changing the character of an area.

Infinite space, or landscape, is where the space extends to the horizon. Buildings are a background element or hidden completely (see figure 1-7) and are never the center, as with negative space. The horizon represents the boundary of the space.

Planes

Walls

A wall is a mass that is a two-dimensional plane rather than a three-dimensional volume. Walls can be freestanding, connected, or an extension of a building. Walls may be used to divide a space into multiple spaces. In architectural design, the term is used for interior partitions that enclose rooms. Dense plantings of vegetation can also serve as walls (e.g., the New Zealand hedge in figure 1-8).

Screens

Screens are partly transparent walls, such as a wrought iron fence. A row of trees can serve as a screen, but it is unlikely to form a wall since you can see in between them (see the street trees in figure 1-9). Screens serve much the same function that walls do in that they can be used to define spaces. The difference is that they do not necessarily fully enclose, as there is usually some visibility through them. Depending on the screen's opacity, it will provide different levels of enclosure (a hedge versus a tree row, for example). The speed of the viewer also affects the apparent degree of opacity. A row of trees on either side of a road operates as an effective screen for passengers in a car, but not for a pedestrian (see figure 1-10).

Floor or Ground Plane

The ground plane—natural or man-made—serves as the floor for all types of environments. Just as in a building, the treatment of the ground plane is an important design element. It can be designed to move traffic, provide space for activities, or preserve resources. The texture of the ground plane is very important (see page 18). The treatment of the floor can direct people or views, make distinctions between spaces, or add interest (both visual and tactile).

Ceiling

All spaces have a ceiling plane, whether it is natural sky, a vegetative canopy, or man-made, such as a constructed roof or ceiling. In architecture the ceiling is a design element similar to the ground or floor. The sky is the ceiling plane for planning, and its juncture with buildings, trees, or the horizon is important to design.

Skyline

Urban planner and architect Edmund Bacon talks about buildings meeting the skyline[4]—a visual line created by the outline of buildings against the backdrop of the sky (see figure 1-11)—as an important urban design element.

Horizon

The horizon is nature's equivalent of the skyline. The horizon may be at eye level and created by the curvature of the earth, as at the seashore (see figure 1-12) or in open landscapes. A horizon created solely by the curvature of the earth is about 2.9 miles distant for a person standing on the ground, and can be called the "natural horizon." Topography and the position of the viewer change the distance to the horizon.

A *borrowed horizon* is when mountains or hills can be seen rising above the natural horizon. The Rocky Mountains, for example, can be seen from as far away as fifty miles, leaving invisible miles of land between the mountains and the point where the earth's curvature would place the horizon. Principally a

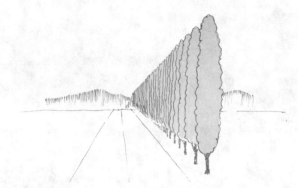

Figure 1-10. Screen parallel to direction of movement creates a nearly solid barrier when moving rapidly.

Figure 1-11. Skyline: where buildings meet sky.

Figure 1-12. Horizon.

Figure 1-13. Borrowed horizon from distant mountains.

Figure 1-14. Artificial horizon where trees rise above natural horizon. Orange County, North Carolina.

Figure 1-15. Tree canopy creates roof.

phenomenon of mountain regions (see figure 1-13), it enables the viewer to borrow a very large distant object that is located beyond the natural horizon.

An *artificial horizon* is the false horizon formed by vegetation that blocks the view to the natural horizon. The artificial horizon can serve like a wall and create small spaces (see figure 1-14). Like a wall, it can be used to hide what is behind it.

Roof

The roof or ceiling encloses a space and is a built element of the environment. For the most part this is important only in architecture, but it is a term used by planners when discussing enclosed pedestrian spaces such as arcades or malls.

Canopy

The branches and leaves of trees form a type of roof (see figure 1-15). While the sky may remain visible above the trees, the sheltering of streets, spaces, or yards by trees is somewhat similar to a roof. Its ability to rise above buildings and alter scale makes it a very important design element.

Scale

There are a number of types of scale, all of which relate to size. Community scale deals with a continuum of scale. Relative scale is a comparative measure of building or space. Human scale relates buildings and spaces to the human, while social scale relates these elements to functions and communication.

Community Scale

Discussed in more detail in chapter 2, this is a measure that distinguishes the scale of a community, from the smallest (the hamlet) to the largest (metropolitan areas). While scale can be expanded to the region or megalopolis, planning is largely absent at these sizes. Population or dwelling units are used to measure community scale.

Relative Scale

Relative scale can simply compare the scale of two buildings in height, volume, or even human-scale units. A new building that would be twenty or more times larger than those already in the neighborhood would be out of scale with its surroundings (see figure 1-16). The term can also be used to compare spaces in terms of area or volume. This is a simple mathematical measure, using height, volume, or the human-scale unit. An important scale relationship is that between spaces and the surrounding buildings (see the section on D/H ratio, page 31).

Human Scale

This term relates to the scale at which a building, room, or space should be created for human use. Rooms and spaces that do not fit the desired activity will be uncomfortable. A stair whose risers or treads are too high or too broad is difficult to climb. Figure 1-17 updates the Leonardo da Vinci drawing to provide a human-scale unit: a six-foot square, ten feet high (or 360 cubic feet). The ten-foot height makes the measure more compatible with zoning standards (ten feet is a common floor-to-floor height in residential buildings). This can be used as a volume measure or, in one or two dimensions, to provide a constant scale. The Japanese, in their traditional architecture, referred to rooms by the number of tatami mats that were used in the modular flooring system.

Social Scale

Spaces have been classified as intimate, personal (or informal), social, and public.[5] But there are other scales that should be added in order to have a system that works from urban to rural character. Five levels will be used here—intimate, informal, formal, event, and infinite. These spaces increase in size and are related to the types of activities that are appropriate.

Intimate scale: Small spaces are intimate. In such a space, individuals are in contact with all their senses and have little room to maneuver to increase their distance. Their faces may be only inches apart.

Informal scale is sized for the comfort of a gathering of friends. People can stand or sit so they can concentrate on the faces of those with whom they are speaking. There is sufficient room for people to move around to talk to different groups within the space.

At the *formal scale,* there may be a key center of attention, or it may simply be a large gathering. With a key focus, a

Figure 1-16. Relative scale between buildings.

Figure 1-17. Human scale: 360 cubic feet.

separation between the gathering and the center of attraction is required. For large gatherings there is no one focus, but the space must be large as people need to be able to form many small groups and move around to different groups. Individuals can be recognized at a distance, though facial expressions and details are lost and conversation is only possible when people break into smaller groups.

Event scale: Events involve very large groups and spaces. These are likely to be facilities for a concert or sporting event. The size of these spaces is such that individual people may be seen, but not recognized, across the space.

Infinite scale: The distances are so great at this scale that people and even vehicles may not be seen until they approach. At this scale even a community with many buildings is seen only in the background.

QUALITATIVE TERMS

Quality is very important in community design. Qualitative terms may indicate a "good" or "bad" aspect of the building or space. In other cases they may be neutral terms describing a characteristic, such as color or texture. Some, like scale, define a social quality of the space. In many cases, there is a continuum involved. The designer needs to be able to use these elements in a knowledgeable manner.

Contrast

Contrast—the opposition or juxtaposition of different forms, lines, or colors—is a desirable feature in human environments and is required in order to maintain interest. A contrast continuum exists, ranging from no contrast to extreme contrast. Unlike some continua, the good is in the middle, with the extremes generally considered undesirable. The states along this continuum are monotony, harmony, and chaos. It can be applied to whole communities or selected elements, homes, colors, heights, textures, or developments.

Monotony is an absence or near absence of contrast. While such an environment has unity, its lack of interest makes it boring or unmemorable. When applied to a neighborhood of homes, individual units lose any sense of identity, and it is difficult to maintain orientation because there are no changes in the environment (see figure 1-18).

Chaos results from too much contrast, and is the opposite extreme of monotony. When every element of the environment is competing for attention, it overwhelms the senses. Strip commercial areas are often chaotic. The corporate architecture, signs, and jumble of building types and styles confuse and clash (see figure 1-19). These strips are not found to be attractive, largely because of this sense of chaos. While chaos is considered to be undesirable, there are exceptions. In Las Vegas or New York's Times Square, chaos is intentional: bright, gaudy, lighted signs obscure the buildings but create a sense of activity and excitement.

Harmony is in the middle of the contrast scale and is the most desirable. It represents a balanced degree of contrast, with unifying elements sufficient to hold visual interest while not being so dramatic as to become unbalanced (see figure 1-20). Note that massing, roofs, and general architecture can achieve this without a rigid style. Unity might also be used to describe this middle ground. Thomas Thiis-Evensen uses the term "continuity" to address the same general concept.[6]

Dominance is an interesting term within the contrast vocabulary.[7] Contrast of a substantial degree may be deliberately used to convey a hierarchy or level of importance. A contrasting element is singled out as being dominant. The medieval cathedral contrasted in height, scale, and style from the rest of the community, visually identifying the dominant social force. Figure 1-21 shows how the height of a steeple gives emphasis to a church in Savannah, Georgia. Government buildings often have a similar dominance due to their scale, height, or architectural features. Dominance should only be planned for a building or space that is particularly important to the community.

Rhythm

Rhythm in architecture or design describes a regular repetition or movement. Examples include movement in a skyline or the repetition of similar buildings. A rhythm can provide a degree

Figure 1-18. Monotony: buildings all the same. Florence, South Carolina.

Figure 1-19. Chaos: building-and-sign overload. Flagstaff, Arizona.

Figure 1-20. Harmony: variety and interest. Serenbe–Chattahoochee Hill Country, Georgia.

Figure 1-21. Dominance: the much-taller steeple focuses attention. Savannah, Georgia.

Figure 1-22. Rhythm: change in second story. Libertyville, Illinois.

Figure 1-23. Texture: mowed lawn and prairie grass. Long Grove, Illinois.

of regularity or alternately provide interest, accents, or contrast (as seen in figure 1-22, where the upper floors are varied). It tends to be a relatively small-scale tool for a large building or block. Maintaining a pattern over many blocks becomes very difficult and potentially monotonous.

Texture

Texture implies tactile sensations. Pedestrians can feel different pavement textures or touch varied building surfaces. It is also a very important visual description applying to things too distant to touch, but whose surfaces are visually different. Texture occurs along a continuum from smooth to rough. The range varies depending on the material being discussed. It is purely a descriptive term; there is no best or worst texture.[8] Texture applies to a range of scales, from small to quite large, and can be used to describe a wide variety of design elements. In figure 1-23, for example, it provides contrast between the mowed grass and the prairie. Pavement surfaces vary from smooth to rough, over a distance of less than an inch. Building fasciae or surfaces range from flat to several inches, and grass from a half inch on a golf green to six to eight feet for prairie grasses.

Color

Color is another basic descriptive term that is of value in manipulating the built environment. There are some areas, such as Cape Cod, Massachusetts, and many areas of Europe, that have a well-established color scheme. Whether it is stone, weathered wood, paint, adobe, or brick, color can serve as a unifying element. It can also be used to provide contrast, either on the individual building, as in the case of trim colors, or to a whole block. Given the array of color choices, it is among the most subtle variables.

Architectural Style

For much of history, style remained constant for long periods of time. The style often reflected limitation in materials. A succession of styles emerged in the United States in the nineteenth century, whereas in the twentieth century there were far fewer styles. The limits imposed by locally available construction materials have largely been eliminated, resulting in residential-construction imitations of styles that are often poorly done. Style is a personal preference. It can create a unifying element or, as with the case of highway commercial areas, approach chaos.

ORGANIZATIONAL DESIGN TERMS

The terms in this section describe either concepts of design or relationships between various elements of the built environment. Some of these terms have very specific meanings—axial, sequential, hierarchical, and symmetry. Other terms are more conceptual in nature—pathways, nodes, edges, and entrances or gateways.

Axial Space

In design, axial refers to a straight street or way between two points intended to make use of perspective as a major structuring element. Specific buildings, monuments, or other structures are laid out at the ends of the axis. The view to the ends is important, so relatively flat land is required. The viewer is strongly oriented to look up or down the axis. The structures at the ends may be important or merely designed to be the visual focal points (see figure 1-24). The axis relies on one-point perspective, in which the perspective makes the buildings, roofs, and bases lead the eye to the structure at the end of the axis, thereby encouraging one to move toward the structure.

This type of design is powerful because it is so obvious and easily comprehended. Radial street patterns typically have multiple streets radiating from one or both ends of an axis. Axial arrangements work best when the design controls what happens along the street from end to end.

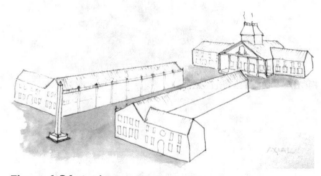

Figure 1-24. Axial space.

Sequential Space

Sequential space is an organizational concept that concentrates on a dynamic changing of the view (see figure 1-25). There may

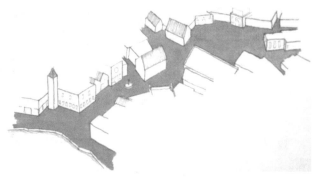

Figure 1-25. Sequential space.

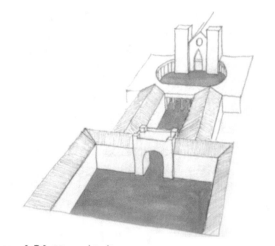

Figure 1-26. Hierarchical space.

Figure 1-27. Symmetry.

or may not be specific endpoints as with an axis. Any endpoint will be changing and may even be invisible at times due to topography or turns. If there are not specific destinations, it is the dynamics of changing views and spatial conditions that is important. The sequential approach can take advantage of all types of perspectives (one-, two-, and three-point), and changing it along the route provides the interest. This type of space works best with an organic street pattern, as opposed to a grid.

Hierarchical Space

Spatial arrangements can also be viewed as some form of hierarchy. Both the axial and sequential arrangement may take this form as well. It assumes that there is a destination objective at one end of the street. The hierarchy can take a wide variety of forms and can even be as simple as the progression from a large space to a more confining or enclosing space and then into a building (see figure 1-26). The opposite may also be used when the final space is intended for large groups; it can serve to distinguish the function of the spaces, such as a progression from public to private.[9]

Symmetry Types

This term explains the balance of building, view, or spatial arrangement. There are two types of balance: symmetrical and asymmetrical. There are also unsymmetrical buildings or spaces, where there is no balance around the center.

Symmetry is a very formal organization. In its purest form a building or space will be identical on either side of a center point when viewing it straight on (see figure 1-27). For buildings this will be seen in the facade. Spaces are different and require control of all sides of the space, with entrances at the same points and facades being balanced.

Asymmetry occurs when the various elements are not identical but are nevertheless balanced. Achieving this balance generally requires considerable design effort. Good asymmetrical design implies balance, as shown in figure 1-28 with a tall building next to a long, lower building. An asymmetrical balance relies on a dynamic harmony achieved by the size, height, mass, and spacing of different portions of the facade.

Something that is *unsymmetrical* lacks symmetry and balance. This is not a negative statement, but simply an indication that the building is not balanced around some axis or viewpoint. Unsymmetrical buildings or spaces are by far the most common situation in communities, since balanced buildings or spaces require more planning.

Figure 1-28. Asymmetry: Tall building balanced with longer lower building.

Pathways

Pathways are the channels[10] by which citizens move through their communities, and from which they view their communities. Streets, pedestrian walkways, and greenways are all pathways. In general, the pathways are roads, sidewalks, or pedestrian precincts that penetrate blocks or move between buildings (see figure 1-29). Paved plazas and squares offer unlimited freedom to walk in any direction and are thus nodes (see below), while parks and campuses often have paved paths intended to direct movement.

Figure 1-29. Paths: several streets and bridge. Beget, Spain.

Nodes

The term "node"—a center of activity—can be applied at several scales; it may be viewed as a point, a corner, or an area. A statue, fountain, obelisk, or single building, such as a church, can serve as a node for a small area or neighborhood. A shopping district or CBD can also be a node on a community, district, or sector scale. A neighborhood as a whole may be a node, such as a town center. At the community level, nodes are generally activity centers for shopping, employment, or entertainment (see figure 1-30). While nodes need space, they are not only a design element: the space must fit the community's needs[11] or it will be abandoned or poorly used.

Figure 1-30. Node at city hall. Bad Tölz, Germany.

Edges

An edge is exactly what it appears to be—the outer limit of the community or neighborhood. Edges can be defined by a wide

Figure 1-31. Edge: river and wall. Besalu, Spain.

variety of elements, such as man-made or natural barriers (see figure 1-31). They may also be defined by changes in land use or character. One of the most important aspects of an edge is that it must be obvious. Edges give clarity to a community, and therefore should provide clear dividing lines. When an edge is unclear, it is difficult to identify when one enters or leaves the community or neighborhood.

Entrances or Gateways

These are just what the words imply: the points at which people enter or exit a community or area. Historically, entrances in walled communities were vividly clear because they were fortified gates (as can be seen at the end of the bridge in figure 1-31). Entrance is another term that can be applied at a wide range of scales. They may be very small-scale, such as the entrances to individual buildings, or slightly larger-scale, such as entries to open spaces. Neighborhoods and nodes should have entries. At the largest scale is the entrance to a town or city.[12] Entrances are important because they contribute to a sense of identity.

LANDSCAPE TERMS

All development occurs initially in a landscape or environment. In terms of design, there are three major topical areas of interest: landforms, land cover types, and landscape types. These terms allow for a description of local or regional differences in environments. The designer must adapt designs to the site conditions. Landforms, land cover, and landscape describe different types of terrain, vegetation, and natural spaces, respectively.

Landforms

Landforms describe topographic conditions. The five landforms are flat, undulating, rolling, rugged, and mountainous, and each describes the texture of the landscape. Visual elements change as the landforms become rougher. The scale of the topographic changes within a landform ranges from inches per mile (flat) to thousands of feet per mile (mountainous). Underlying geology may affect local appearance.

Flat

This landform has little change in elevation, with very gentle and nearly invisible slopes—little different from the horizon at sea. In the absence of tree cover, buildings will be seen penetrating the skyline. Slopes will be measured in increments of a foot or two on most properties and tens of feet to the horizon.

Undulating

In undulating terrain the land is typically divided into low valleys created by the drainage pattern. The slopes are still very low (with a maximum grade of less than 3 percent, or three feet in one hundred), and the elevation differences from ridge to valley floor are generally low as well. Where there is a clear view to the horizon it will still look very much like a straight line. On the small scale, ridges are inadequate to hide or screen buildings. Like all other terrains, undulating terrain can occur on a small or large scale.

Rolling

Steeper slopes and more elevation changes are found in rolling landforms. Here the term "hill" will come into use in a meaningful manner.[13] Small-scale rolling terrain can have significant variation within even a small farm field. At a large scale there may be wide river valleys. Rolling and subsequent landforms take on a different character depending on the position of the observer: on a ridgeline, as in figure 1-32, the horizon is miles away; from the valley floor, as in figure 1-33, the ridge acts like an artificial horizon and may be less than a mile away.

Figure 1-32. Rolling land from ridgetop. Palouse terrain, Whitman County, Washington.

Figure 1-33. Rolling land from valley floor. Palouse terrain, Whitman County, Washington.

Rugged

This is often found in mountain chains where erosion has worn down the peaks and filled the valleys. It is often folded into many ridges and valleys. The slopes can vary from modest to very steep depending on the local features, but from the valley bottoms the horizon is highly elevated. Crossings of ridges are limited so valleys become separate communities. Again, scale is important; rugged land may occur along major rivers in otherwise flat land where stream valleys have cut into the landscape.

Mountainous

In truly mountainous terrain, the vertical drop from peaks to valleys can be thousands of feet. These are nearly all in the western United States. The scale of these features is very large. While valleys within the mountains can be very steep, there are often large valleys with mountains on both sides. Mountains can only be crossed by way of passes or with extreme expense (such as blasting a road through), as there are extremely limited natural crossing points.

Ridges and Valleys

The undulating terrain of ridges and valleys can be either very small-scale or large-scale. In mountainous terrain, some valleys are little more than a streambed, while in other cases they may be miles across between mountain ranges.

Land Cover

Land cover refers to the natural vegetation or second growth (since much of the nation has been cleared). There are a number of major cover types: forest, savannah, prairie, desert, and farmland.

Forest

Forests or woodlands are areas where the vast majority of the land is covered by tree canopy. Visually, objects even a little way into the distance are invisible from the outside.

Savannah

This is a mix of trees and grassland. The trees are so widely spaced that only small groups have touching canopies.

One can see a considerable distance into the savannah because there is little in the way of understory to block the view.

Prairie

Prairie or grasslands are a landscape dominated by grasses and other forbs. There are three levels of texture involved with prairies or grasslands. The tall-grass prairies have vegetation from five to more than eight feet in height. Short-grass prairie is much sparser in cover, often with nearly open ground visible and average vegetation heights of one to two feet. Old field or meadow grasslands generally have grasses that are eighteen inches to four feet in height.

Desert

In the United States these areas are concentrated in the West and have a distinctive desert biota that exists on very little rainfall. It can range from virtually barren soils and rock to deserts with large cactus that can exceed twenty feet in height. There is no real canopy vegetation.

Farmland

Farmland in field crops, vegetables, orchards, or pasture all falls into this category. Pasture and prairie may be indistinguishable in many parts of the country. Similarly, orchards may take on some of the characteristics of forest or savannah.

Mixed

In many areas there will be a mix of forest, woodland, grassland, or agricultural land covers so that there is a pattern of open fields and areas of trees. Tree rows or trees along water courses often break up open areas.

Landscape Types

Vegetation, like buildings, is capable of creating space or landscape types. The distance/height ratio (D/H, see page 31) used for urban spaces can also be a measure of natural enclosures (e.g., open spaces surrounded by woodlands or tree rows). In a great many environments, vegetation significantly alters the perception of space.

Infinite Space

This occurs when land is open to the horizon. While topography may hide areas, the skyline is always open land, with no landscape mass.[14] This space is found in flat to rolling landforms, but is also experienced on ridge-, hill-, or mountaintops where the horizon is uninterrupted.

Undifferentiated Spaces

In these spaces, where there may be only a distant tree line within sight, there is no visual sense of enclosure or defining a space. The tree line will appear as only a thin line at the horizon. The D/H of undifferentiated spaces is in the 150–300 range.

Defined Spaces

These are spaces that have artificial or false horizons, such as tree rows or a forest edge, that create visual boundaries to the space. Defined spaces have D/H values from the viewer to the artificial horizon in excess of forty. At the low end of this range, as seen from the center of the space, fifty-foot trees in the tree line appear to be nearly two feet in height due to perspective when compared to a fifty-foot-tall foreground tree. The degree of enclosure is similar to a low hedge in an urban situation.

Enclosing Space

While the D/H is still high in enclosing space (over sixteen), the artificial horizon or forest begins to create a space that is visually a meadow or field surrounded by trees.

Enclosed Space

The clearing in the forest has a D/H between two and ten. These spaces are similar to urban spaces, except that the enclosing walls are forest or woodland rather than buildings. Enclosure in natural settings is achieved at higher D/H values than in urban settings due to the nature of the space being open land rather than a pedestrian activity area.

Forest Edge

This is not a space, but the boundary area at the edge of a woodland or forest. It extends about two hundred feet on either side of the tree line. It is an area important to design for rural character and, as such, is different than the edges discussed above.

Buildings a little way into the forest edge are well screened, and buildings next to the edge are more easily screened.

Interior Space

Interior space here is much like the interior space in a building; the viewer sees the tree canopy as a ceiling much as a ceiling in a building. The canopy arching over buildings and roads creates a very different environment, altering the relative scale of the buildings because the trees are taller. A small clearing with D/H of up to 1.0 will not lose its forest character.

Articulated Space

All the spaces discussed above assume that there is a regular enclosure of spaces, from extremely large to very small. The landscape is often organized into fields by tree lines or woodlands, creating a series of linked spaces of varying sizes and shapes. The result is somewhat akin to sequential space in urban environments. The space can be dramatically different depending on the direction one is looking.

LAND USE AND ZONING TERMS

Planners and zoning specialists use a whole different language from that of the designer. It is critical that the terms be measurable. It is unfortunate that land use and density, the most common elements, are very poor measures of character or quality. There are other measures that have varying potential for insuring a desirable community character, such as open space ratio, building coverage, floor area ratio, impervious surface ratios, and landscaped surface ratios. Some are fairly common, while the profession only rarely uses others. Because of the need to relate the zoning regulations to community character building, the measures of building volume ratio, landscape volume ratio, and site volume ratio are very valuable.

Land Use

Land use, which is the primary component of most comprehensive plans and zoning, addresses the use of a building or land.

There are four general use categories: residential, commercial, business (office and industrial), and agriculture/parks/open space/vacant.[15] These categories quickly get broken into individual land uses, such as fast-food restaurant, clothing store, art gallery, and so forth. The concept of use can get very detailed and complex, as with the federal land use code system, which has over fifteen thousand classifications.[16] Detailed classification of land use is not important in defining character. Of the eight community character types, only two (agricultural and natural) are distinguished by land use. As will be shown in chapter 3, most commercial and business uses can be designed to achieve any of four or five character types. Thus, land use does not determine character.

Intensity

Intensity measures the extent or impact of the use or activity in a space, parcel, or area. Comprehensive plans typically measure residential density in broad terms—high, medium, and low—and assign density ranges. Zoning generally considers density or a surrogate, such as lot area or size. Other intensity measures deal with the coverage or floor area of buildings and are better suited for nonresidential uses. Measures of impervious surface or open space are very important in defining the environmental impact of development.

Lot Size

The first zoning ordinances controlled the intensity of development by regulating the minimum area of a lot and frontage on a street, and most still do ninety years later. The creation of a series of zoning districts with different minimum lot sizes provided different intensities. The application of lot size has resulted in what is known as cookie-cutter zoning.[17] Unfortunately, too many planners and citizens view lot size (or density) as a holy grail of land use planning. Citizens often see lower density as better, which has contributed to sprawl.

Density

Density measures the dwelling units on an area of land. It is measured by dividing the number of dwelling units on a property by its acreage, and is stated in dwelling units per acre (see figure 1-34). Some citizens have trouble dealing with decimals, so some planners use acres per dwelling unit when density is less than one dwelling unit per acre (which is not density, but rather lot area per dwelling unit). There are several variations on density, determined by the area used in the calculation. Density can be very misleading in terms of the character that is created. Most important, a good designer can increase density yet still maintain or improve character and quality.

Gross density is calculated using the total area of the development site.[18] This is the density actually achieved on a site by a developer, including land allocated to lots, streets, and various types of open space (see figure 1-34). As such it is the preferred density measure because it accounts for the entire development.

Net density uses the area of lots and roads, but excludes open space. This measure has less value, since most developments (except in larger cities) have open space requirements for detention of storm water that can range from 5 to 20 percent of a site. It also ignores wetlands and floodplains. Many comprehensive plans use this measure, which is not good because it overestimates the yield that can actually be achieved by development.

Net-net density is a density measure that includes only the lot, and excludes land in streets and open space. This is the closest one comes to the minimum lot area as a measure of density. It has little value except to discuss the density of the built-up area or housing type.

Building Coverage

The building coverage is the portion of the lot or site that is covered by the building, as shown in figure 1-35. While this has often been used, it cannot distinguish between single- and multi-story buildings.

Floor Area Ratio (FAR)

This is the ratio of the total floor area of a building to the size of the land allocated for that building (see figure 1-36). FAR is the equivalent of density for nonresidential uses, but can be used as a bulk regulation in residential districts instead of setbacks. The FAR was developed in response to the inability of building coverage to assess the impact of buildings with

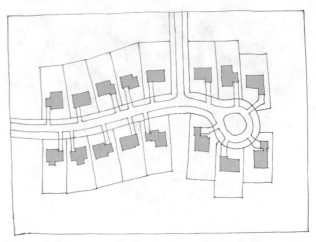

Figure 1-34. Density: dwelling units per acre.

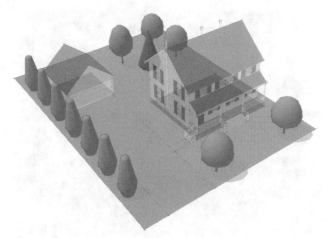

Figure 1-35. Building coverage.

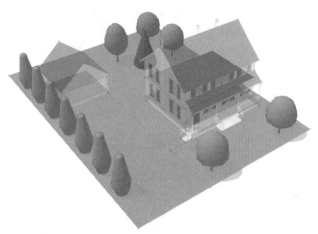

Figure 1-36. Floor area ratio.

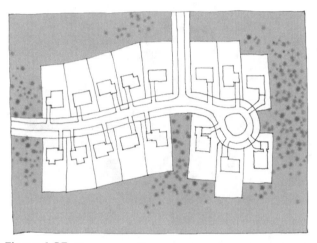

Figure 1-37. Open space ratio.

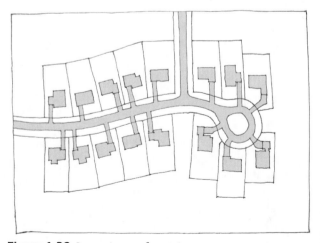

Figure 1-38. Impervious surface ratio.

multiple floors. A one-story ranch and two-story house with nearly identical building footprints would be nearly 100 percent different in FAR. The FAR is always a positive number, but unlike many other ratios, it can exceed one. Its only failing is that it is not effective when floor heights are very different.

Open Space Ratio

This is the area of the site that is in open space divided by the total area of the site (see figure 1-37). This measure is designed to focus on real, public-type open spaces; it excludes land in the minimum required yard areas and rights-of-way. It is a lower value than pervious surface or green space, which include land on lots and in rights-of-way. It is used to protect natural resources as passive open space, community recreational land, detention, or buffer yards. Open space ratios will range from 0 to near 1.0 (100 percent).

Impervious Surface Ratio

The impervious surface ratio was developed primarily for environmental reasons. It measures the area covered by buildings and paved parking lots, roads, and loading areas, divided by the total area of the site (figure 1-38). It is important to both storm-water runoff and water-quality analysis. But it is useful as a measure of land use intensity as well. It accounts for some of the areas that are not measured by either building coverage or floor area ratios. In defining what constitutes an impervious surface, some flexibility is needed. Unpaved parking and loading areas and exterior storage, regardless of whether they are truly impervious, are often included because of their pollution potential. This measure's value ranges from 0 to 1.0.

Landscape Surface Ratio (LSR)

This measure is relatively new,[19] and could be called the pervious surface ratio. LSR measures the ratio of landscaped area to the total site area (see figure 1-39). LSR is a very different measure from open space ratio, because it includes lawns and landscaped rights-of-way. The sum of the landscaped surface ratio and impervious surface ratio is one. Because nonresidential areas do not normally have open space, the landscape surface ratio substitutes for it as a measure in these areas.

Distance/Height Ratio (D/H)

D/H is a measure that has long been used by architects to measure enclosure. The distance across a space (D), divided by the height (H) of the surrounding buildings, results in a numeric value that is the degree of enclosure (see figure 1-40).

There are several rules of thumb about the enclosure of positive spaces. In general, a D/H of less than one means a very enclosed space. As space increases or buildings or walls become lower, the degree of enclosure is lessened. D/H values of four or five approach the threshold for what can be considered an enclosed space; above this value, a loss of enclosure will be experienced.

Horizontal enclosure addresses the degree to which buildings surround a space. Many urban spaces approach 360 degree enclosure, with only street accesses providing breaks. This is measured in the degrees, with 360 degrees being fully enclosed. Only a few urban spaces would have as little as 270 degrees (open on one side).

Figure-Ground (Building Coverage)

The figure-ground has been used at least since Camillo Sitte's *City Planning According to Artistic Principles* in 1889. Architects use it to visually represent the city by showing the buildings in black and everything else in white (see figure 1-41). Geographic Information System maps often have a buildings layer, and thus can be developed to provide a visual measure of the difference between urban and natural environments. It is a useful way to distinguish some of the community character types. A variation on this would be color parking or landscaped areas.

Volume Measures

All the prior measures are two-dimensional and thus fail to consistently measure the bulk of development. Three measures were developed to provide a more accurate description of community character: building volume ratio, landscape volume ratio, and site volume ratio.[20] A fourth, the human-scale measure, was covered earlier in this chapter (to recap, it relates a building or space to a volume six feet on a side and ten feet

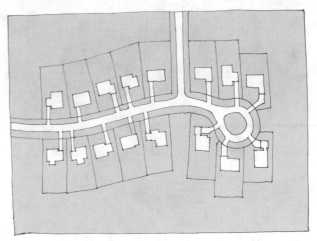

Figure 1-39. Landscape surface ratio.

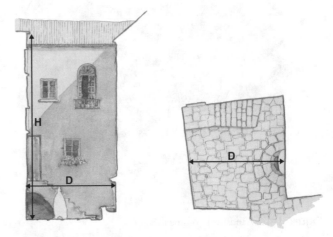

Figure 1-40. Distance/height ratio (D/H) measures enclosure.

Figure 1-41. Figure-ground.

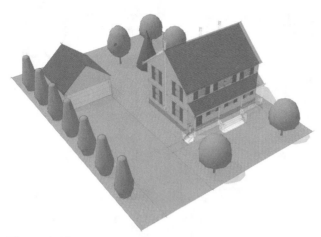

Figure 1-42. Building volume ratio.

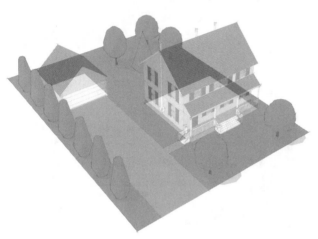

Figure 1-43. Landscape volume ratio.

high). Another measure, the plant unit, was developed to estimate the future volume of landscaping.

Building Volume Ratio (BVR)

The building volume ratio is a measure of the volume occupied by the building plus that occupied by parking, loading, and exterior storage (see figure 1-42). The building volume is divided by ten and then divided by the area of the site. The division by ten seeks to make it numerically similar to the floor area ratio.[21] This measure corrects an important failure of the floor area ratio. For example, a ten-thousand-square-foot, one-story office building and an automated warehouse could have identical floor area ratios but very different volumes; the office building will be fifteen to eighteen feet in height, while an automated warehouse may have interior spaces that are fifty feet high, giving a building height of fifty-four to fifty-six feet and thus three times the bulk. The floor area ratio also suffers from its inability to address other aspects of development such as parking, loading, or exterior storage yards. The fact that engineers and architects can all calculate volume on their computer systems eliminates the complexity of dealing with varying shapes.

Outdoor storage areas have a volume that should be calculated based on the largest objects they'll be used to store. At-grade or surface parking lots are assumed to have a height of five feet, higher than a car but lower than vans and sport-utility vehicles. Loading areas are calculated at a height of twelve feet to account for tractor trailers.

Landscape Volume Ratio (LVR)

The landscape volume ratio is analogous to the building volume ratio except that it measures the volume of the landscape present (see figure 1-43). The landscape volume is in direct contrast to the building's volume or mass, and may serve to hide buildings. The area and height of the canopy serve to measure existing tree stands. It is more difficult to measure landscape. The area covered by trees is multiplied by the height of the canopy to determine the landscape volume. The area covered by trees is divided by ten and then by the site area to create the LVR.

Site Volume Ratio (SVR)

The site volume ratio allows a total characterization of a lot or street scene that relates both building and landscape volumes. It is calculated by subtracting the building volume from the landscape volume. This means that both positive and negative values are possible, and that they have intrinsic upper and lower limits. The result is positive when the landscape volume is greater than the building volume. A negative number results when the building volume is the larger of the two. Figure 1-44 illustrates the use of SVR to compare developments. In these four sites, three existing developments have positive SVR values, and the proposed development has a negative SVR; thus there is a clear change in character that is measurable.

The advantage of this tool is that it is a composite measure of two very important volumes that alter the character of the site. For example, two buildings might have similar BVRs, but if one has little or no landscaping the SVR will be negative, while a similar building surrounded by trees will have a positive SVR. The density or land use might be identical, so the SVR is very powerful.

Plant Unit

LVR offers two challenges: first, how to measure new landscaping from a plan; second, how to deal with the growth of plant material. One can measure the volume of each tree and multiply it by the number of trees, but that is a time-consuming exercise. The plant unit is a mix of canopy, evergreen, understory, and shrubs, which can be conceived of as a solid mass when planted in a forty-by-forty-foot area. Figure 1-45 shows several options for a plant unit. The plant unit can then be the basis for landscape requirements. If a lot requires two plant units, it is then easy to calculate the volume. The height of the plant unit is crucial; since trees are young when planted, the practice is to assume canopy trees of thirty feet in height, which occurs between ten and twenty years after planting. A useful rule of thumb is that approximately twenty-five plant units per acre are needed to create a woodland (see figure 1-46).

COMMUNITY CHARACTER WORD USAGE

In creating a system of community character I was troubled by a limited vocabulary, in which one word had multiple potential meanings, such as "rural," "suburban," "urban," or

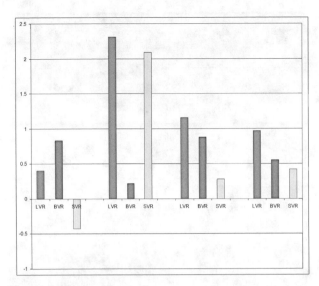

Figure 1-44. Site volume ratio.

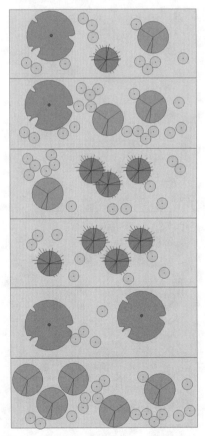

Figure 1-45. Plant unit alternatives.

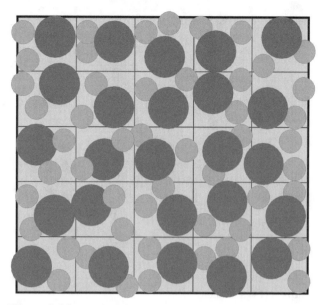

Figure 1-46. Number of plant units (25) per acre to create a forest.

"community." The following is the language of community character. These terms are described in more detail in the following chapter.

Community/Municipality

In this book, "community" will be used to refer to the scale of a community that is defined by its economic sphere, and "municipality" will refer to a political jurisdiction. This distinction is needed because in metropolitan areas, municipal boundaries often have nothing to do with how economic activity is organized. Even in a town surrounded by a rural area—a freestanding community—there may be development in the surrounding unincorporated land, and the market area may extend miles beyond the town limits.

Sub-urban/Suburban/Suburb/Suburbia/Slurb

There are a number of distinctions that need to be made with these words. First, a class of character will be designated as "sub-urban," while "suburban" is used for one of the two character types in the class ("estate" is the other). There was a time when city and suburb could clearly be described, so that both geographical location and character would be clearly understood. In this book, I use the term "suburb" or "suburbia" to distinguish the geographical meaning from the character description. In metropolitan areas, what is now geographically suburbia is an intermingling of urban, sub-urban, and even rural character types. The form found in suburbia might better be called a slurb, a scrambled and confused agglomeration of character types (typically suburban and auto-urban; see chapter 3).

Rural/Countryside/Agriculture/Natural

This was the easiest area because I was able to distinguish the constituent rural types from the rural class with three separate words. "Rural" is the overarching class, which is comprised of three types: "countryside," "agricultural," and "natural." Rural is also used to describe regions, portions of states, or groups of states where the economy is food- and fiber-driven and agriculture is the dominant use of the land.

Urban/Auto-urban/Urban Core/Urbanization

This proved to be the most difficult. There are three types of urban within the urban class of character. "Urban" must, unfortunately, be used for both the class and one of the types. I will try to use "class" or "type" at the beginning of a discussion, but it will not be done for each usage. "Auto-urban" and "urban core" are the other urban character types. "Urbanization" will be used for the process of converting rural land to either an urban type or sub-urban type.

CONCLUSION

The lexicon should assist in understanding the various architectural, planning, zoning, and community character terms used in this book and in *A Guide to Planning for Community Character*. It also provides a common vocabulary with precise definitions.

2 Community State, Context, and Scale

Community state and scale are systems of classifying human settlements as to their physical relationship to other communities (state) and their size (scale). Not only are these descriptive terms valuable in classifying a community, but they also have value in planning for the future. The scale of communities relates to the economic and cultural potential, as well as the potential for problems such as congestion. A community is defined by its economic and social functions, rather than its political boundaries. Municipalities are political entities, while communities are functional elements. Municipal boundaries often have nothing to do with economic functions; markets ignore them, choosing instead to look to the area. In both cases, the boundaries are largely invisible on the ground.

There are two possible states for a community: freestanding and composite. *Freestanding* communities are those where the settlement or built-up area of the community is isolated from other communities by an expanse of rural land. *Composite* communities share their edges with other communities. Community-scale boundaries are nested, as a community contains several internal neighborhoods. Municipal boundaries also share edges with other municipalities, but these rarely relate to community economic boundaries. It is common for an economic community to encompass residents of several municipalities. For freestanding communities, the municipality is the settlement that we might call a village or town, but economically it serves the surrounding rural area and population. A regional mall is the commercial center of an area containing many municipalities.

Scale measures size using population or dwelling units, rather than using a land measurement. Both community state and scale can be represented together on a tree diagram with two branches. Unlike tree diagrams that show the evolution from

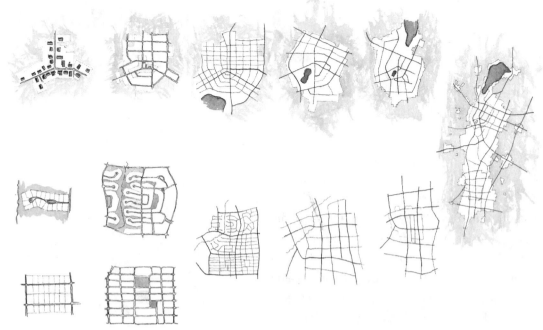

Figure 2-1. State and scale: freestanding (*top*) and composite (*bottom*).

the starting point of the trunk to the tips of the branches, the scale diagram begins at the outermost ends, with the smallest-scale unit of development at the end of each branch. Also, each branch is the same length and has the same number of scale levels. As a community grows in size on either branch (freestanding or composite), it moves along to the next scale level (see figure 2-1). At the largest scale, the branches merge to form a metropolis that includes both freestanding and composite communities.

Regions are very large and can cover portions of states as well as multiple state areas. There are three regional contexts: rural, independent, and metropolitan. *Rural* regions have an agricultural base served by widely dispersed, freestanding municipalities. *Metropolitan* regions have a central city along with communities that are located in closer proximity. *Independent* regions have a mix of agriculture along with small cities and suburbs that are relatively isolated. The regional types have very different economies.

Planning is done for the future and generally implies growth. Most communities want to grow, and this is almost a given in metropolitan and independent regions. This is another area where a distinction needs to be made between municipality and community. In metropolitan areas, many central cities (municipalities) may lose population while the metropolitan area grows; in many of the shrinking cities there is often a net gain in dwelling units (although the experience in the recent recession may be an exception).

In rural regions, there are declining communities, stable communities, and some that are growing. While municipalities have no choice about what region they are in, in order to plan realistically it is important to understand the context within which the planning must occur. The economics of the three regional types are very different, as are their general growth prospects. Preserving freestanding communities is also sensitive to regional context. It is common to see a goal or vision statement calling for the preservation of "small town" character. That growth from village to city will destroy the "small town" should be obvious. A change from freestanding to composite is also a clear indication that the "small town" value is likely to be lost due to the increase in size and population. Composite communities that attract regional-scale uses can also destroy their character by attracting commuters and shoppers from many municipalities. The change from freestanding to composite is irreversible, so the community that undergoes this state change will become a component of a larger community.

Community size is a much better measure of character than municipal size. A small municipality may have the metropolitan area's regional mall instead of the much larger central city, but it also must cope with the traffic that use creates.

COMMUNITY STATE

Since "state" describes a community's physical form in its relationship to other communities, a community's state is recognizable on the ground or from the air. On the ground, the rural land surrounding freestanding communities provides a clear sense of where the community begins and ends. Leaving the rural area indicates that one is entering another community. The settlement or nucleus is urbanized (urban or sub-urban) and surrounded by landscape (see figure 2-2). The boundary between the settlement and surrounding rural area is very clear and distinct in this aerial view.

Figure 2-2. Freestanding community. Door County, Wisconsin.

Figure 2-3. Composite community: road and density divides two neighborhoods. Palm Beach County, Florida.

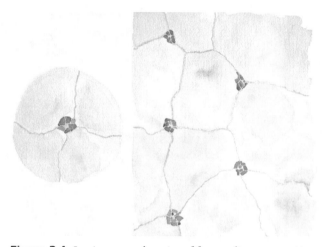

Figure 2-4. Service area and spacing of freestanding communities.

There is no rural land area separating composite communities. While there are small areas of vacant or agricultural land, it does not provide a sense of separation; the community abuts others. Figure 2-3 shows a composite community where two neighborhoods with very different densities border each other. These and other developments behind them form a composite community (see figure 2-12 for multiple municipalities).

Freestanding Communities

The maintenance of the rural (agricultural or natural) land that separates freestanding communities is essential to their character. Planning to maintain a freestanding character requires both control over the municipality's growth and the use of the rural land outside the municipal boundaries.

A good way to visualize a freestanding community is to think of it as a cell, with the nucleus as the settlement. The nucleus settlement[1] is surrounded by a rural area (the cytoplasm), as seen in figure 2-4. The settlement boundary is what is seen as the community boundary, and is likely to be close to the municipal boundary. The economic area the community supports goes out to the cell boundary. The spacing between settlements is the sum of the radii of the economic service areas of the communities. It is important to note here that the settlement or nucleus of freestanding communities comprises smaller units, just as in the composite community. It is the surrounding rural land that distinguishes the freestanding community.

A freestanding community must make a decision on whether it desires to remain freestanding and take action to avoid having another community grow into it (or vice versa). In rural regions the lack of growth makes the threat minimal. In independent or metropolitan areas the threat is real. There is nothing to stop one community from annexing up to another; in fact, it is actually encouraged by competition for taxable land. Even development in the unincorporated area can transform the state from freestanding to composite without two municipalities touching.

Edges

The edge of the settlement is very important in providing the community with a clear image and a sense of place. Medieval hamlets, villages, and towns were walled communities, as seen in the German town in figure 2-5. These walled medieval towns were often built on defensible hills that provided a very hard edge (as in the case of Orvieto, figure 2-6). The importance of a sharp edge cannot be overemphasized. As one approaches a community, a hard, sharp edge gives a clear entrance experience and prevents sprawl. Even without a wall, most European towns, villages, and hamlets retain a hard edge (e.g., Beget, Spain, shown in figure 2-7). While the hard edges may have once been a defensive measure, today they are planned to retain agriculture and freestanding character.

If a community sprawls out, its risk of growing together with another community is greatly increased. Too often in the United States a community has no hard edge, and commercial uses sprawl outward along major roads (as shown in figure 2-8). This has many undesirable consequences. First, a sense of entrance is lost, as it is unclear when one has arrived. Which is the entrance: the first building along the road, the municipal boundary sign, or an area with solid development on both sides of the road? Sharp boundaries are visually superior. They also are beneficial in controlling the surrounding rural area that protects the community's freestanding character. The municipality can control growth within its boundaries, but cooperation is needed at the edge because the rural land is usually in the control of the adjoining township or county, or worse uncontrolled because of a lack of zoning. Controlling the edge and rural area is the central challenge facing planners who seek to maintain a freestanding community.

Another damaging aspect of sprawl is the location of commercial uses along the major roads, which weakens the center by encouraging disinvestment in the downtown. The sprawl also lengthens trips. Adding to the damage is the fact that these uses are often of low quality (see figure 2-8) and diminish the impression one has of the community. Commercial uses often extend beyond the residential areas, so views of open land are lost before one enters the community. Unregulated signage, billboards, stripped residential lots, and occasional commercial have visually blighted the rural character of many freestanding communities. The area shown in figure 2-9 is part of a strip where, for six miles outside the town, there is never a point where a sign is not visible, destroying all unobstructed views of the rural landscape.

Figure 2-5. Edge: fortified wall and gate tower. Rothenburg, OT Germany.

Figure 2-6. Fortified city edge on hilltop. Orvieto, Italy.

Figure 2-7. Sharp edge fitted to topography. Beget, Spain.

Figure 2-8. Sprawl along highway. Florence, South Carolina.

Figure 2-9. Sign sprawl six miles from town. Door County, Wisconsin.

Figure 2-10. Un-zoned, scattered residential in rural land. Flathead County, Montana.

Exurban residential development disrupts the nature of a freestanding community. The rural landscape is replaced with homes that consume a great deal of land for the population they support. Strip development along rural roads is visually the worst of this phenomenon, but any low-density development can be damaging because it is destructive to the rural landscape and takes away from the sense of a freestanding community (figures 2-10 and 2-11).

Separation

What is adequate separation between freestanding communities? There is no hard rule on this. There are certainly models that can be found by looking at the traditional, agriculturally supported communities, which were spaced by travel time for the farmers on foot or horse and wagon. The speed of automobiles condenses the apparent separation from an hour or two to minutes, but is measured in miles. The ratio between rural area and total area should approach 100 percent, with the settlement occupying less than 1 percent of the service area. Topography, physical barriers, vegetation, and type of agriculture can all modify spacing between communities. In general, the spacing found in rural areas today provides some guidance (see the discussion of measurement in chapter 5).

A community that wishes to remain freestanding must first carefully plan for limited growth and then detail considerations of the character type they would like for that growth. The denser the character type selected, the greater the possible growth with a limited conversion of rural land. This is not easy planning, but failure to do so means becoming a composite community. Not only does protecting freestanding character require local effort, but regional planning is needed to encourage the cooperation of other local governments.

Composite Communities

The composite community at a large scale is a twentieth-century phenomenon. In 1820 only ten cities had populations in excess of ten thousand people.[2] At the beginning of the twentieth century the United States was still a very rural place, with a large percentage of the population employed on the farm. These farm populations were supported by hamlets, villages, and small towns—all freestanding communities. Only a small population lived in composite communities. The fact that there is no transition between composite communities requires a totally different way of thinking about identity, sense of place, or entrances to a community. It is more challenging to have a distinct community character, so it is important that municipalities think about this issue early. The incremental aspect of growth forces planners to concentrate on each subdivision rather than on neighborhood or community identity. This leaves the issue of community identity without an advocate until its absence is seen as a problem. Thus planners need to anticipate the growing together of communities and plan to create a municipal or neighborhood identity, even when the community is still freestanding. Once two communities grow together, they cannot revert.

The fact that municipal boundaries are not related market areas, and that boundaries are irregular, makes planning more difficult. A decision of one municipality or private-sector entity to seek annexation encourages irregular boundaries. A regional mall or employment center nearly always has a market area that extends well beyond the municipal boundaries. Thus, while one municipality may reap huge fiscal advantages from sales tax revenues, the communities that provide the center's shoppers or workers do not share in the benefits. This is discussed in more detail below.

Identity in Composite Communities

In freestanding communities, the rural land creates a clear sense of identity because the communities are separated. How does the planner or architect work with citizens to create an identity for a municipality or neighborhood in composite communities? Identity is a sense of place for the neighborhood or municipality. It is about recognizing the difference between two adjoining neighborhoods or municipalities. Local government has largely failed to provide clear neighborhood or municipality identities for composite communities. The character of land along a major highway, for example, is too often continuous auto-urban, with nothing more than a boundary sign that would distinguish one municipality from the next.

Developers have opted to abandon both the neighborhood and city to give identity to the subdivision or gated community.

Figure 2-11. Estate sprawl. Laramie, Wyoming.

Figure 2-12. Composite area with multiple municipalities. Palm Beach and Martin Counties, Florida.

Unfortunately, they do this by spending money on the entrance to their development, giving it a name, and attempting to limit its connection to neighboring property. This is bad for connectivity and lessens the residents' identification with their neighborhood or municipality. The gated community is the most destructive form of this developer-driven identity because it represents a barrier to neighboring, communicating, and traveling within the larger community. It can lead to segregation rather than the unification of a neighborhood or municipality. Restricted entrances increase trip length by turning developments into cul-de-sacs.

Whether it is a neighborhood or municipality, the issue of identity within the composite community is a major challenge. Where is the community in figure 2-12? The photograph shows an area in two counties and three municipalities. There are no visual clues from the air unless the boundary follows the river. On the ground, only road signs would identify the boundaries. How does one achieve identity when there is only a property line, street, or line on a map to create a boundary? Figure 2-12 shows three types of edges: roads, a very sharp change in land use, and a river. Setting good boundaries is important, and different elements are effective in different conditions.

Boundaries

Roads can be logical boundaries for communities. Large roads work because they are a visual edge and a barrier that must be crossed to the adjoining community, as was shown in figure 2-3. Heavily traveled roads, such as arterials or major collectors, present social barriers, since the traffic volumes make it difficult for pedestrians to move from one community to another. All too often arterials are lined with commercial uses, which screen the residential neighborhood from view. The commercial strip is highly undesirable in creating neighborhood identity. This suggests that the boundary of the neighborhood should have relatively the same use and character as its interior. Eliminating the strip commercial requires that some neighborhoods be of mixed use to accommodate the commercial services. Having an edge barrier created by a completely different environment or land use from the rest of the community, as illustrated in figure 2-13, is destructive because it gives a false impression of the character of the larger community behind it. On

Figure 2-13. Land use edge, car dealer against residential. Jupiter, Florida.

the other hand, if the land use is different (residential and commercial) on either side of a major road, then the two areas have established different identities. Ideally, long strips should be broken into nodes; composite municipalities could then use residential differences and landscaping to distinguish themselves, as was the case with the townhouses and single-family units in figure 2-3.

The best composite community boundaries are natural; they create real separation, which provides identifiable entry points. It is far easier to enhance or maintain ten entrances than it is to deal with eighty. Streams and floodplains are ideal boundaries. Because floodplains should be undeveloped, they punctuate the differences in land use or character types. At the border, a green space provides a great opportunity to create a sense of leaving and entering, even if it takes only a few seconds to cross. A natural area provides a visual break and permits residential units on an edge to borrow views of open space.

Changes of land use or density at municipal or neighborhood boundaries are good ways to create identity. There should be a landscape buffer that protects the lesser-intensity character type, as was shown in figure 2-3, where both buffers and roads define neighborhoods. For municipalities that intend to create identity and avoid adverse impacts, planning for edges is important.

COMMUNITY SCALE

Scale is a measurement of the size of the community using population or dwelling units—the standard measurements for growth. Both should be used, since population per dwelling unit changes over time. For example, in the 1970s family size declined and the census showed some communities losing population while the number of dwelling units increased. Either population or dwelling units provides a number that translates to market potential. Population is an important measure of the feasibility of commercial and service-business location decisions. A business needs a population base of sufficient size and wealth to support it (in terms of workers and customers). The availability of cultural and health facilities is highly related to population. An increase in scale is driven by growth, thus scale changes are critical to transportation and infrastructure planning.

The idea of scale was conceived to distinguish differently sized communities and better understand, plan, and organize them.[3] Community scale focuses on the economic and social aspects associated with each of the six levels of community scale: hamlet/block, village/neighborhood, town/community, small city/district, large city/sector, and metropolis (which includes both freestanding and composite states).

Table 2-1 presents the scales for both freestanding and composite communities. Note that there are several criteria that

Table 2-1. Community scale

Freestanding	Hamlet	Village	Town	Small city	Large city	Metropolis
Composite	Block/cluster	Neighborhood	Community	District	Sector	Metropolis
Population	25–875	1,500–4,000	7,000–13,750	20,000–50,000	100,000–625,000	1,000,000+
Dwelling units	10–350	600–1,600	2,800–5,500	8,000–20,000	40,000–250,000	400,000+
Area	4–140 ac.	200–533 ac.	1–5 sq. mi.	10–30 sq. mi.	50–250 sq. mi.	400+ sq. mi.
Regional character	Rural independent	Rural independent	Rural independent	Independent rare in rural	Metropolitan	Metropolitan
Rural character (freestanding)	Yes	Yes	Yes	Rarely	Only at edge	Only at edge
Internal character available	Estate, suburban, auto-urban, urban	Estate, suburban, auto-urban, urban	Estate, suburban, auto-urban, urban	Suburban, auto-urban, urban	Suburban, auto-urban, urban, urban core	Suburban, auto-urban, urban, urban core
Uniformity of character	Unitary	Unitary with node possible	Some variety	Variety	Diverse	Diverse
Function (freestanding)	Crossroads	Rural service	Rural service	Rural center	Regional center	N/A
Function (composite)	Building block	Basic residential unit	Complete community	Supports many communities	Major support center	Metropolitan complex
Economic role	Vestigial, hamlet	Convenience	Community	Subregional	Regional center	State or national
Land use	Residential	Residential with local service	Mixed	Mixed	Mixed	Mixed
Cultural diversity	Very low	Low	Modest	Moderate	High	Very high
Social network	Part of larger	Full interaction	Too large	N/A	N/A	N/A
Health care	Too small	Too small	Individual practitioners	Hospital	Large range of facilities	Large range of facilities
Transit suitability	Too small	Bus stop	Rail stop	Supports a small system (bus or light rail)	Supports a large system (bus and rail)	Supports a large system (bus and rail)

apply to only freestanding communities (regional type and rural character). The description of function is different for the two states. A gap has intentionally been left between each level in the scale to indicate that there is not a precise point of scale change, but rather a gradual transition. One additional person does not change a hamlet into a village. There will be a transition stage where it is unclear whether a community is a hamlet or village. The gaps are needed when a community wants to retain a specific scale. In such cases there will need to be a maximum well below the lower limit of the next-higher scale's lower limit.

The economic impact of scale is strongly felt in freestanding communities. A resident of a small freestanding community will need to travel long distances to find retailers that are readily available in metropolitan areas. These shopping options are not available locally because the limited market cannot sustain them. In small towns and villages of the western plains and mountain states, for example, residents may drive hundreds of miles for services or shopping.

Because composite communities abut each other, there is no relationship between community and political boundaries in terms of economic function. Businesses locate based on transportation and economic considerations. For shopping, families go to highway businesses, local convenience stores, community stores like supermarkets, and regional centers. Employment is likely to range out to a twenty-plus-mile radius. The mismatch between municipal boundaries and economic ones creates a situation where there are winners and losers, because some communities get windfalls of revenues based on a commercial center that is actually supported by residents of many other communities. While local government may want to claim that their planning achieved this, it is far more likely that regional transportation-improvement decisions provided the impetus by creating a location that the market wanted. Regional planning decisions that more evenly pool and redistribute tax revenues are needed (see, e.g., the work of the metropolitan council in Minneapolis–St. Paul). From the design perspective, a framework for planning borders is needed.

It is possible to create a total mismatch of goals and land use plans. For example, a large land owner in New Castle County, Delaware, proposed the development of three new villages following the New Urbanist model. The land developer's plan called for more than one million square feet of commercial and four million square feet of office and industrial. This is close to the size of an edge city.[4] The three villages put together would not have a population large enough to support this level of commercial and regional employment, and the land use would be totally dependent on commuters. The daily automobile traffic these uses generate would destroy the nature of a small freestanding village, where one can walk everywhere and socialize with their neighbors.

Scale provides a way for communities to consider goals such as quality of life and match them against the effects of a particular land use. In the example above, matching the desire for a village-scale environment with a major regional shopping or employment center is shown to be incompatible.

Hamlets and Blocks or Clusters

The hamlet (freestanding community) and block or cluster (composite communities) are at the smallest scale, with populations of 25 to 875. At this level, there is a profound difference between the freestanding hamlet, which is a true community, and the block or cluster, which is only a building block for a neighborhood (except at the most extreme densities of urban cores).

The freestanding hamlet, whatever its physical form, was an economically independent community until very recently. Historically, it was often a farming community where people lived and worked in the surrounding rural land, with a small business community that served the hamlet residents. In this country, where farmers live on their farms, it was a support center for a surrounding farm population. As such it had a strong social structure and some form of economic activity. This economic element is vestigial in many historic hamlets due to changes in shopping, marketing, and transportation in the last century. A new hamlet is unlikely to have an adequate market base. Figure 2-14 illustrates a hamlet where residents work the surrounding farmland. The hamlet, because it is freestanding, is characterized by the prominence of its edge conditions, where the built-up area ends and rural land begins. In most hamlets, the majority of the community consists of development that is one lot deep—a single lot between the street and the surrounding rural area. Thus they have a tremendous perimeter-to-area ratio, with few if any interior units. Traditional hamlets normally do not have blocks, but large or new ones could.

The hamlet design is strongly influenced by the road pattern on which it is structured. The hamlet will be more compact when located near crossing roads than when strung along a single road or shoreline. In designing a new hamlet to provide for rural living, the one-lot-deep design provides maximum views into the surrounding rural areas. Even when the hamlet has several blocks, individual structures will not be far from the surrounding rural land.

In the composite community, the block or cluster is the basic building block from which larger-scale units—neighborhoods—are organized and constructed.[5] Blocks are surrounded by streets and organized into groups (see figure 2-15). Clusters may be oriented around a cul-de-sac or loop street, can be in groups, and are typically surrounded by open space (see figure 2-16). The individual block or cluster is not an independent economic unit because it is too small. Socially, it is also too small, because neighboring occurs across the street to the next block, rather than only with those who live to the side or rear on the same block. The block created by surveyors to prepare land for sale has had a profound impact on the American landscape. In the nineteenth and twentieth centuries, curvilinear blocks were developed for new communities, and cul-de-sacs came into greater use. In the suburbs, clusters may be separated by open space, thereby enhancing neighboring within the cluster where the street is included.

Villages and Neighborhoods

These are the second scale level, and both comprise many blocks or clusters, having populations of 1,500 to 4,000. At each successive scale level, the higher level has multiple lower-level units. As a hamlet grows, additional houses are added along the original streets and new streets are added, creating blocks, and over time it will evolve into a village (see figure 2-17). Internally, the village is a composite form, consisting of multiple blocks or clusters. Both freestanding and composite states are now

Figure 2-14. Farming hamlet. Mekong Delta, Vietnam.

Figure 2-15. Curvilinear blocks. Sturgeon Bay, Wisconsin.

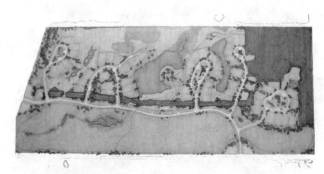
Figure 2-16. Cluster plan. Fields of Long Grove, Long Grove, Illinois.

Figure 2-17. Fishing village. Port Clyde, Maine.

functional economically, whereas blocks or hamlets may no longer function. The neighborhood is the level at which neighboring and social interaction within the scale level work. Above this level, work or common interests trigger socializing, not physical proximity. The same generally holds true for the village, but because of their isolation, freestanding communities have stronger economic potential than the settlement population would indicate. Both the village and neighborhood are still able to support some commercial activities, but in many cases at a substantially reduced level due to changes in retailing that favor new business models and larger market areas.

The connections of the village to other villages or towns are roads leading through open country to the next community. Neighborhoods share common boundaries; visiting or shopping in another neighborhood normally would require only the crossing of a street. Even though they require careful design, it is unusual today for a neighborhood to be conceived as a unit, except by very large-scale developers. Most comprehensive plans are silent on the design of neighborhoods. Thus a neighborhood is likely to be a group of subdivisions built by different developers over time. This can create problems for the cohesiveness of the neighborhood by limiting access and creating barriers.

In physical terms, communities at the village and neighborhood scale should be walkable, which suggests a radius of 1,320 to 1,500 feet; this results in about a ten- to twelve-minute walk through the neighborhood.[6] Estate areas will be much larger, but travel by bicycle easily duplicates the travel time of pedestrian areas. Table 2-2 shows the impact of character type on the area for a village or neighborhood of 4,000 people (or 1,600 dwelling units). Maintaining these distances may be difficult because the existing rural road pattern often creates the basis for the arterial and major collector network. As communities develop on the fringe, the farm roads offer access. In much of the West and Midwest, one-mile-square units of land (called sections) can be divided into quarter sections to create road spacing of 2,640 feet (3,734 feet from corner to corner of the quarter section). At any suburban or urban intensity, these roads often become major collectors or arterials, which—depending on density—may be four or more lanes. The arterials and collectors

Table 2-2. Community character type and area

Neighborhood or village: 4,000 people, 1,600 dwelling units

Character type	Density	Radius (ft.)	Area (ac.)	Area (sq. mi.)
Estate	0.4	6,600	4,000	6.25
Suburban	2.8	2,494	571	0.89
Auto-urban	5.5	1,780	291	0.45
Urban, low	8.0	1,476	200	0.31
Urban, high	12.0	1,203	133	0.21
Urban core	60.0	542	27	0.04

are used for subregional and regional trips. These roads define superblocks, in which all the internal streets are local streets providing access to individual uses. This keeps regional traffic out of neighborhoods. The section pattern means that as density increases, the quarter section roads may need to be arterials to support the higher traffic volumes.

One element that should be present in all villages and neighborhoods is park land. Be it a formal park or a greenway, there is need for neighborhood recreation. Villages may logically use land on the periphery of the settlement for park land because of the freestanding nature of these communities.

Because of the importance of the neighborhood as a basic unit for socialization, along with its historic importance, a section on neighborhood design is included in comprehensive plans. Neighborhood models from the early twentieth century are completely outdated.[7] The automobile has totally altered access to shops, services, work, culture, and recreation. When those models were developed the pedestrian ruled, with transit being used primarily for work trips. The lack of refrigeration in the home meant near-daily shopping trips. Neighborhoods were traditionally anchored by the corner store, church, and tavern/restaurant. Jobs are spread throughout most metropolitan and independent regions, and now most families have two people in the workforce. Shopping for food is no longer a daily necessity, and the trip must nearly always be made by car. The local house of worship has lost its neighborhood identity and now serves a population scattered across a community of larger scale; thus instead of walking, the parishioners come by automobile. A new neighborhood model is needed to reflect the realities of twenty-first-century employment, business, and culture.

Neighborhood Design

The neighborhood is a composite community abutting other neighborhoods. Many people approach the neighborhood as having a fundamental place; Nelessen, for example, characterizes it as a central retail and civic space.[8] This is little different from Unwin's designs in the late nineteenth century, which likewise were oriented toward a center.[9] Both these approaches are clearly modeled after the village or freestanding town from 1890 to 1930, which makes them poorly suited for current conditions. The village's commercial and institutional center was usually located near the crossroads that provided access to the community. It was the logical place for commercial—central to everyone. The central business location of neighborhoods presumes that the residents walk to shop. The corner store is dead except in high-density urban areas; people demand more choice than the corner store offers and only shop once or twice a week, factors that are unlikely to change.

The anchor store that is sustained by the population of a neighborhood is the drug store. This is a building of about fifteen to eighteen thousand square feet, which now serves traditional drug and pharmacy needs, but also has elements of the convenience store. Other retail and service uses are small, including dry cleaners, beauty and barber shops, tanning saloons, real estate offices, and other small businesses, with all other uses being generally less than two thousand square feet.

It will be a rare neighborhood center that needs more than twenty to thirty thousand square feet of floor area, requiring less than three acres of land. This means only a small block is needed. Mixed residential and commercial is desirable. Because of the convenience nature of the businesses, the limited size of stores or uses does not create a problem.

Businesses prefer to be on major roads because of the traffic volume and visibility. The major roads should not run into the center of the neighborhood. Experience has shown that bringing major roads or even collectors into the neighborhood creates conflict. Residents do not want the traffic passing their homes and therefore agitate for traffic calming and stop signs, which runs counter to the interests of business owners, who want visibility to the highest volumes of traffic. Traffic calming prevents high traffic volumes and lengthens trip times, and thus is poor transportation planning. It is far better to consider other locations for commercial.

There are two logical options. The first is to move it to the edge of the community, where there is access and visibility from the major road. The second option is that commercial nodes be located at the intersection of four neighborhoods, which enables more and larger commercial uses. This provides greater market potential and places the node at the intersection of two major roads, which for commercial is a preferred location. This leaves the neighborhoods to be almost exclusively residential. The one option that should be rejected is turning the major roads into strips (as discussed above).

Parks should either flow through the neighborhood (if there is a natural feature that logically promotes this) or be near the center. When elementary schools served their neighborhoods exclusively, a central location made sense. Today most elementary schools serve several neighborhoods, and should therefore be located to minimize traffic intrusion into the center of a neighborhood.

Today a great number of neighborhoods have one housing type and density. Care needs to be taken not to create design differences that split the neighborhood into two units that have different characters and social interactions. The neighborhood is the largest unit where the entire population can have a unified social interaction, and that must be encouraged. A diversity of residential options is easily achieved within a community character type, as type is not dependent on use or lot size. This provides for a far greater range of housing opportunities within the neighborhood for families with changing needs at different stages of their lives.

From a design perspective, neighborhoods require a strong identity. The neighborhood borders are a logical place to establish this identity. The neighborhood generally has a major collector or arterial road that establishes its perimeter. The positioning of blocks with respect to perimeter streets is important. The ideal is to have the short side of the blocks face the arterial border streets, so that as one is entering the neighborhood, side yards provide a suitable buffer between the homes and major roads. The long block face means that the individual homes front on major roads, creating conflict with traffic flows unless access to these units is by alleys. The short blocks are safer, because cars do not have to back into a busy street, and children are less likely to play near the arterial than the local roads. Having both a sidewalk and bicycle path on the edges can enhance the entrance. Making developers create a common neighborhood entrance feature is also a desirable approach to creating neighborhood identity.

The arterials that border most neighborhoods pose a nuisance for residents, therefore designers should seek to mitigate the problem. A variety of tools are available: greater setbacks from arterials, landscape buffers, walls, reverse frontage roads, and the design of the arterial cross-section are methods to be applied singularly or in combination to insulate residential from high-traffic volumes.

Towns and Communities

A town or a community, the third level of the scale, comprises three to seven neighborhoods and has a population of between 7,000 and 13,750 (see figure 2-18). One of its neighborhoods is likely to be a central business district (CBD). This area would ideally provide for the weekly commercial needs of residents, allowing this scale to be relatively self-sufficient. As an historical example, of the three thousand communities in the Holy Roman Empire, no more than fifteen had a population in excess of ten thousand.[10] The last one hundred years have seen a huge change, however, as many towns are transitioning to the next scale level.

The concept of specialized neighborhoods for the CBD, which can be seen in most rail suburbs from the late nineteenth and early twentieth centuries, is still valid today. All the specialized neighborhoods need arterial access, as well as special border treatment to protect residential areas. Parks, natural features, or landscaping features are useful as buffers. All the districts should have a good mix of uses. Commercial and residential is a desirable mixed use, as the residential reduces trips and supports the commercial. The level of business activity allows the mix of uses to really have an impact, as the central area has a sufficient market to benefit from the retail and strengthen the central area against outlying competition. Offices, heavy retail, hotels, restaurants, and industry provide a good mix of uses for

Figure 2-18. Town. Provincetown, Massachusetts.

employment areas. Residential should not be included because truck traffic poses a hazard. Only heavy industries are generally incompatible uses in employment areas. The creation of nodes or neighborhoods for central business and employment has much to recommend it, in contrast to the strip approach, where uses are strung along major roads, creating economic competition for the town or community center.

Most towns or communities will have multiple character types within their boundaries. The full range from urban to estate is possible, as is a mix, but the choice is a local one. The average character type has changed from urban to suburban in the last hundred years. Energy consumption, global warming, and changes in the workforce and family composition are all factors at work today that may again alter the mix. In metropolitan and independent regions, it is fair to say that the freestanding town is an endangered state.

The town or community center serves all its constituent neighborhoods. The larger population base provides a greater market, supporting large stores with more goods and permitting some more specialized uses than are found in villages. This carries over to more cultural opportunities, such as museums or theaters. Small town character and a close-knit community are highly valued and are threatened by growth. Community character is stronger in freestanding communities than in composite ones due to the isolation created by the rural areas surrounding them. But caution is needed in romanticizing the small town values because they have limitations. For example, Japanese, Greek, or other ethnic cuisines are often not available. Businesses have greater limitations for walk-in traffic or even efficient shipping. The anchor stores for such communities are supermarkets and large hardware stores. At the upper end of size, an occasional freestanding town might get a big box in rural regions because its location allows it to serve a market that includes other freestanding communities, as well as the area's farm population—but the town itself does not have the population to support it. The limitations on the town do not transfer to the community that abuts other municipalities, since it is part of the higher-scale levels.

The town is the upper limit for where the average resident still feels much of a connection to the surrounding rural area. Unless a resident commutes to another rural community, only those on the edge of town see the rural area daily.

Figure 2-19. Small city center. Dubuque, Iowa.

Small Cities and Districts

Small cities and districts are the fourth level in the scale, with populations of twenty to fifty thousand. The distinction between municipality and community is largely lost, because even a freestanding "city" is likely to comprise the central city, suburbs (often municipalities), and unincorporated development. The central city municipality is in the interior of a multi-jurisdiction composite community that is a single economic unit surrounded by rural land. A district may be a part of many municipalities. Economically, however, the multiple municipalities are a unit, a fact that is often not appreciated by municipalities. A small city should have at its core an economic engine that concentrates jobs and retail, likely in its CBD (as shown in figure 2-19). A district should also have a central place, but this is less likely, as each municipality may have its own downtown, and strip development further weakens such a possibility.

Over the past fifty years, the centers in a great many municipalities of this scale have seen a decline, along with increased activity on major roads. In the past, the anchor tenant of the area was a small department store in the CBD. Too often those have failed or have been driven out, and the replacement anchor store is a large discount retailer like Wal-Mart, located toward the edge of the city. This still leaves a small city's residents with a significant lack of shopping opportunities for quality goods, forcing them to travel long distances (one to two hours each way) to find additional opportunities. This is not true in the case of districts, because they are part of a sector that has the regional center within twenty minutes. Major chains may be found at the upper end of the sector population range, thus increasing the availability of goods.

In order to avoid having a high flow of commuters, residential needs to be balanced with shopping and employment. At this scale there is an increase in economic, social, and cultural diversity sustained by populations of between thirty and seventy-five thousand people. Today's small city or region has as its core a subregional commercial and employment center. That employment-commercial center could and should be highly concentrated in a small part of the city or district.

There are very few American communities of this scale that do not have a mix of sub-urban and urban types. Diversity in housing and economic opportunity is to be encouraged. A population of this size means that there will be families who need nearly all the urban or sub-urban housing types. While a specific, average community-character-type image may be desirable, caution is needed to not overly limit housing opportunities or character types and force these people out of the area. Such an action would encourage sprawl, which wastes energy, creates longer trips, and drains talent and expertise from the community. It is unwise to force uniformity of character type at this scale.[11]

While the small city may provide services for surrounding rural areas and even many rural villages, the resident loses a sense of connection to the surrounding farm community that exists at lower-scale levels. This occurs because the average resident does not experience the rural areas unless he or she leaves town. Worse, the residents of the central city municipality are likely to be cut off from the rural area by suburbs, so preserving the rural boundary is an even more remote issue. The problem of sprawl into the rural area is likely to be more challenging as there will be multiple political jurisdictions that have to take unified action.

Large Cities or Sectors

The large cities or sectors, like their smaller brethren, are nearly always composed of multiple political jurisdictions. The scale of these communities ranges from 100,000 to 625,000 people. Note that the population range for cities at this scale would result in a metropolitan area designation by the Census Bureau. Although located in rural regions, cities like Spokane, Washington, or Jackson, Mississippi, take on a character that is totally independent of their surrounding areas. Spokane serves portions of two states that are predominantly rural and agricultural. Like Lincoln, Nebraska, Jackson is a state capital, and while serving the surrounding area as a commercial and cultural center, it also has a statewide function. Because of this, most freestanding cities of this size are also small metropolitan areas. They are nearly all found in rural or independent regions, and the economic service area is likely to contain several freestanding communities in close proximity, as well as several growing together to become

Figure 2-20. Large city center. Auckland, New Zealand.

Figure 2-21. City center from distance. Auckland, New Zealand.

composite communities. The sector is the composite equivalent of the large city and is purely an economic element, with a shopping and employment center generally anchored by a regional mall. Even a very large city—like Chicago, Houston, Los Angeles, or New York—contains many sectors within the city limits in addition to the CBD.

Both sector and large city support the full range of commercial, with department stores and every other form of retail (see figures 2-20 and 2-21). This means a core area with well over one million square feet of retail, whether it is in a downtown or peripheral location. In a central location, employment will involve four to six million square feet of space. The sector, which will be found only in large metropolitan areas, has as its commercial center what is known as the edge city—a regional center that fulfills the shopping and employment functions of a large city's central business district.[12] In large cities, one sector will be in the central city. In composite situations, the sector center may fall within the boundaries of several municipalities or even be on unincorporated land. It is important to note that the central commercial and employment functions are only a small part of the larger economic community. Thus the actual commercial center might only be a community-scale node within the sector. In general, there is no planning for sectors because they have no political base. Planning for the sector as a key economic structure in the metropolitan area is a missing element in current planning and should be made a priority; it would better enable these areas to be used to structure a more sustainable metropolitan area and approach to transit.

Metropolises

As cities and metropolitan areas continue to expand, they reach a population of around one million, at which point they become able to support several sectors. The city's CBD and several existing regional centers or edge cities characterize this level. For large cities, there is a central city downtown that is the economic core. Figure 2-22 shows the Boston city center as viewed from the water, which clearly illustrates the central city regional core and how it visually stands out from the surrounding urban areas. While not all cities are fortunate enough to have their core so visually distinct by virtue of a waterfront location, it is important for regional centers to be both visually and economically dominant.

Metropolitan areas are dynamic, growing outward in rings, beginning with the first-ring suburbs. The design problem is how to locate transportation and new edge cities and create a metropolitan form so that the area is not an undifferentiated slurb. As defined in the chapter 1, slurb suggests a low-quality suburb, but it is actually a very good description of a mix of auto-urban and suburban character types whose character is unclear. If growth occurs in undifferentiated rings and radial strips, there is nothing much to distinguish one community from another. The early attempts at regional plans envisioned metropolitan forms; unfortunately, the politics of most regions have precluded any serious effort to implement these forms. The planned retention of rural areas would be to give form and clarity to the metropolitan area. Organization of a metropolitan area must create some area-wide hierarchy of places and clear spatial definitions. It should also create a logical relationship between the various regions.

Figure 2-22. Metropolitan CBD. Boston, Massachusetts.

Megalopolises

There are many areas of the country where two or more separate metropolises form groups with populations of ten million or more. This scale level exists, but it is not included in the scale set. There are likely to be several states in most megalopolises, so it is worth mentioning here. But with no current planning at the megalopolis level, there is no reason to discuss it further.

Regional Planning

Beginning at the small city level, the economic radius of the settlement center will likely include freestanding communities well beyond the central city and its suburbs, and include a number of smaller freestanding communities. This factor becomes more pronounced for large cities and metropolitan areas. The growth at the fringe of freestanding towns, villages, and unincorporated areas results in sprawl that lessens their character.

Unless planning preserves freestanding communities within its growth area, it will simply continue to convert farmland, natural areas, and freestanding places into an ever-expanding slurb, having very little to distinguish any of its municipalities. A planned region can be more attractive if it provides permanent rural areas within its boundaries as it grows. Ideally, that planning will begin at the scale of small or large cities. The greater the diversity and mix that can be created, the greater the potential exists for municipalities to have a clear identity. If regional planning begins early, it will enhance the ability to protect freestanding communities at the metropolitan level. Both annexation and unincorporated development can result in the freestanding community becoming a composite community as the rural land is lost. This is clearly an area where at least two governments are always involved and where regional planning with teeth is badly needed.

Unfortunately, most regional planning agencies in the United States have no legal powers over land use or annexation, and have abandoned the effort to create metropolitan forms. Both the large city and sector involve so many jurisdictions that there is no logical constituency to preserve rural areas. The governments of central cities and suburbs may or may not get along, and municipalities may have conflicting interests. This is where regional planning is even more essential to making plans at this level work. A major constraint is that the municipalities do not share any common interest in the city or sector as a whole. Again, there is no planning agency that has the power to address this, except in the case of some city-county joint governments or other city-county agencies where there is only one political decision maker (e.g., in Minneapolis–St. Paul, Nashville, and Portland). The sharing of resources is important to planning at this level.

SCALE AND ECONOMICS

The scale of communities is closely linked to economic potential, most obviously in freestanding communities. Retail and service sectors of the economy are tied to the population and its relative wealth. A bigger population can support more uses. Thus population growth means increasing economic health. In a community with a stable population, new stores or buildings are built from time to time. But the "new" development is simply moving the same or similar uses from elsewhere within the community or replacing obsolete ones. Office and industry are also related to population, although major employers can move people and facilities—as auto plants, Sears, and Boeing have done—within the region or to other states. The movement of major employers can have adverse impacts on the communities they leave, as well as positive impacts on the communities receiving them.

In this discussion of scale, the focus is on how businesses relate to population. Each use has a minimum population needed to sustain it. A subset of this is anchor retail that attracts numerous other uses to locate around it. The anchor, whether a drugstore, supermarket, or regional mall, is in a node within the market area of the scale unit. The freestanding community will have a larger population than a composite community of similar population. This occurs because the surrounding rural area is populated and worked by farm families. The difference is highly sensitive to the regional population density and the scale level. For the hamlet and village the population is sensitive to the type of farm community, lower in areas of larger ranches (measured in square miles) than in areas where farms are smaller. As one goes up the scale, the difference becomes larger, since the city's economic radius is likely to contain not only the farm population but also hamlets, villages, and even towns.

There is a hierarchy of markets based on the populations and areas they serve. Market levels can be defined as convenience, neighborhood, community, subregional, and regional, and these correspond to the scale levels (see table 2-1). Each of these levels has anchor stores or businesses that become feasible only when the population is large enough to sustain them. There has been a very significant change in the representative uses at these levels from only fifty years ago. This has been driven by the marketplace, technology, and transportation. For example, the average corner store built in the early twentieth century was around 1,000 square feet in area. The midcentury supermarket was 7,000 square feet.[13] The supermarket at 60,000 square feet is now being outflanked by the superstore with 150,000 square feet or more. Commercial businesses remain in a high state of dynamic change, as seen by recent bankruptcies, so the uses discussed are subject to continuing evolution in the years ahead.

The corner store sold a range of products: from meat, vegetables, canned and boxed food, and some clothing items. It was operated by a family who lived above the store and managed it without employees (other than the family members). The corner store's demise is the result of several factors. Our demand for variety and choice requires vastly more space; the candy aisle in a modern convenience store occupies ten or more times the space as it did in the corner store. Today there are few families that would devote the time needed to operate this type of business. The one exception is in ethnic neighborhoods, where newly arrived families can get a start with a small store, and where the immediate neighborhood seeks specialty ethnic foods not commonly found in the supermarket. In metropolitan areas the small stores are far more specialized and also tend to be slightly larger than the corner store. The corner store has in fact evolved to a convenience mart and dropped a number of the traditional foods, while adding automobile products and fast food. Basic food shopping in much of the nation moved from corner stores to supermarkets by the 1950s. Other retail uses—TVs, office supplies, cards, and clothing—have followed a similar trajectory. The level of choice in products has greatly increased, and products from all over the world are sold. Americans have also become fascinated with stuff, expanding homes to accommodate all the goods. A change in size like this must also have a larger population base to support the sales.

Community scale is related to community population and thus to a commercial service level. Each level in the community scale is associated with a market level. The community scale sets limits to the types of services and commercial a community may have. A village cannot support a supermarket, a category killer like Best Buy or Office Depot, or a big-box discounter. There are exceptions to this that are predictable. The highway service industry—gas, food, and lodging—is sensitive to traffic volumes. Transportation routes, interstates, and major arterials create a market that is a reflection of the volume of traffic (and the nature of that traffic) on the road, without respect to the population living nearby. This traffic volume represents a transient population. A village on an interstate interchange has more of these services than its population can support. This effect is most pronounced at the smaller scales. Another predictable variant is the university town or small city. These often cater to a larger service area because the cultural and other activities that come to the university create a market of opportunity that would not otherwise exist. The students and university events draw visitors. These factors combine in a manner that increases the market beyond the community population. Tourist destinations also offer larger markets than their permanent populations would indicate.

There are some uses that buck the trend. Banks have gotten smaller, often with little indoor service. The advent of the ATM takes banking down to the village/neighborhood level. There are some exceptions to the size in rural or independent regions, where there are mostly smaller communities; small supermarkets (thirty to forty thousand square feet) cater to these areas, and uses like a Wal-Mart or a car dealership will choose one of ten communities to serve a large portion of that rural region.

In looking at the market in relation to community scale, the uses have been divided into retail and service categories. Building supplies, category killers, convenience stores, department stores, drugstores, hardware, specialty clothing, and supermarkets represent a fair sampling of retail uses. Service uses include automobile service, banks, dry cleaners, fast food, gas stations, personal services, hospitals, hotels, professional services, and video rentals. These all have their requisite support populations. In table 2-3, these uses are related to the community scale. The nature of the community scale is that the preceding scale level becomes a component of the next. For example, a town or community comprises several neighborhoods, and small cities comprise several communities. Table 2-3 focuses on the likelihood of a use being found as an anchor in any community. The metropolis level is not included, as it just has more of everything than the sector. The uses are rated as follows:

> *Highway*: The use is dependent not on the area's population but on traffic volumes on the road.
> *Low*: A low probability because population is marginal to support the use.
> *Moderate*: Good probability, but the use may be absent.
> *High*: Maximum probability that the use will be supported and present. This rating indicates that the use anchors the commercial area.

Table 2-3. Community scale and common land uses

Land uses	Hamlet/block-cluster	Village/neighborhood	Town/community	Small city/district	Large city/sector
Population	25–875	1,500–4,000	7,000–13,750	20,000–50,000	100,000–625,000
Retail uses					
Building supplies	No market	No market	Low-Moderate	High	Background
Category killer	No market	No market	Low	Moderate	High
Convenience	Highway	High	Background	Background	Background
Department store	No market	No market	No market	Moderate	High
Drugstore	No market	High	Background	Background	Background
Hardware	No market	Low	High	Background	Background
Specialty clothing	No market	Low	Moderate	High	Background
Supermarket	No market	Low	High	High	Background
Service uses					
Automotive service	No market	Moderate	High	Background	Background
Bank	No market	Moderate	High	Background	Background
Dry cleaner	Low	High	Background	Background	Background
Fast food	Highway	Highway	High	Background	Background
Gas station	Highway	Highway	High	Background	Background
Personal services	Moderate	High	Background	Background	Background
Hospital	No market	No market	Low	Moderate	High
Hotel	Highway	Highway	Highway	Background	Background
Professional services	No market	Moderate	High	Background	Background
Video rental	No market	Moderate	High	Background	Background

Background: This category relates to uses that serve smaller communities. The dry cleaner may be a neighborhood use, but there may be hundreds of neighborhoods in a large city, so the use will be found everywhere.

No market: The population is too low to support this use.

At each scale level, the uses with the "high" rating are the anchors of that scale level, the major retail or business attractions. The uses that are high at the lowest levels of the scale are relatively ubiquitous and are present as background uses at higher levels. At the higher levels, planning would suggest that the uses would be found in the community's central core. Unfortunately, that is not always the case. Many communities across the country have let their cores decline and allowed the anchor stores to escape to strips. The growth of central places requires that they constantly renew themselves and expand. In towns across the nation, downtowns of the 1950s contained supermarkets and variety stores, with few larger than ten thousand square feet. The rapid change in size of retail uses has had a terrible impact on central places. How does one redo a downtown—to vastly increase the size of these uses and provide parking (or transit)—in a built-up environment? There are major difficulties in assembly of land, the cost of parking, and dealing with residential areas that want no intrusion; further, the cost and politics of condemnation have always slowed this process down.

In planning, the community scale provides not only the general size of the community, but also a means of checking expectations for reality or plans for impacts on the quality of life. As a town grows to a small city, its requirements for land are not proportional to its growth, because it is serving a larger market, and must also provide for new types of businesses. Understanding this helps focus on the need to expand the CBD as the community grows. While these uses and market areas are relatively fixed at any point in time, they are dynamic and in flux as retail continues to evolve and strive for efficiency. The other trend is that the life expectancy of investments has been shrinking. While buildings are built to last, the investors now want to have made their money in ten years or so. While some uses (restaurants, for example) have little individual impact, others have very large impacts. A regional mall will attract other retail development to take advantage of synergistic effects; thus the impact on roads and taxes is very high. The traffic volume, for example, is so high it can destroy the character of a village or town. Even in a composite setting, the community needs to anticipate the effects of traffic.

Renewal or redevelopment poses the most difficult planning issues. The proposed expansion of a downtown is something that is almost never seen in comprehensive plans. As a result, concern for a downtown's future may only arise after the area has declined. Any growing community with a quality downtown needs to have a renewal, expansion, or redevelopment approach as a basic element of its plan. This generally requires a plan that allows the central area to grow into surrounding areas, in many cases converting residential land to commercial use. The dynamics of change mean that to replace old supermarkets with new ones requires a floor area four times larger and finding a parking area for the customers. The cost of land assembly and the politics of rezoning make this very difficult. For other uses, structured parking and transit are very expensive and require government intervention. If the CBD has adjacent industrial land, that might be a better expansion option. It is essential that most of the uses that have migrated to strips be forced into the CBD and that buildings be allowed to increase in height so mixed use can be sustained. Municipal investment in structured parking and transit is essential to this strategy (see chapter 6).

CONCLUSION

Understanding state, context, and scale is important to good planning. If an existing freestanding community wants its character preserved, there are clear actions that must be taken to limit growth and prevent sprawl into rural areas. Context is generally not changing rapidly, but understanding it should inform decision making. Scale is very important because it is linked to economics and social functioning, which may affect the growth strategy of a community. In any case, scale suggests an organizational concept for communities, and particularly requires more attention be paid to the character of the components, such as neighborhoods. State and scale represent a different way of thinking about a community than does land use.

CHAPTER 3

Community Character Classes and Types

What are the physical and visual attributes of community character? What are the attributes of communities that promote or are essential to the functions and lifestyles associated with each? The fact that these questions are often asked demonstrates a need for a community character system. The three basic character classes of urban, sub-urban, and rural have social, economic, and environmental attributes tied to each. The character types may be converted to zoning districts, thus directly addressing the goal of protecting character, which neither density nor use currently achieves.

While state addresses exterior relationships and scale focuses on social and economic factors related to the size of communities, character classes and types focus on design relationships, such as the intensity of development and the relationship between buildings, spaces, and landscapes. Different aspects of these physical relationships determine the character of an area and control or limit human interactions. Differences in these design elements facilitate or limit the opportunities for social interaction and economic activity. The different character types provide for different lifestyles.

The three principal community classes of urban, sub-urban, and rural have very different functions in life: rural as the producer of food and fiber, urban as a place of trade and commerce, and sub-urban initially as a place of escape from the city. Those functions resulted in very different physical forms and shaped the lifestyle of each. Today, in a great number of municipalities, the functions are mixed so that commercial and employment centers have been moved to suburbs, thereby altering their sub-urban character. In rural areas, use is very important, while it is not a factor in the urban or sub-urban classes. There are some uses, like heavy industry, that do not fit and are not real communities since they are so specialized.

The classical urban character has evolved in cities and towns over centuries. In general, the design rules of architects or planners,[1] when applied, have successfully retained urban character or created new urban areas. These rules use buildings to define spaces (plazas and parks) and streets that enclose and concentrate activity. The spaces have a very architectural character.

Sub-urban environments were places of escape from the city. They have changed and diversified somewhat in form in reaction to changing economic and transportation conditions. Until the rail suburbs began to emerge in the nineteenth century, most sub-urban housing was for the wealthy elite living on large estates. The sub-urban class rejected the enclosure of urban design, instead borrowing views of space from open land or expansive lawns. As a place of escape, the yard—rather than the street, square, or park—became the center of outdoor activities. The automobile had a dramatic impact on the suburban type, making the suburbs a realizable utopia for the working family, instead of an enclave for the rich. This changed the nature of suburbs, which until then were home to a very small percentage of the population. The suburbs first changed to bedroom suburbs, and then brought in commercial and employment centers and came to rival or exceed the population of urban areas. Lewis Mumford writes in *The City in History* that sub-urban areas were "so enchanting that those who contrived it failed to see the fatal penalty attached to it—the penalty of popularity, that fatal inundation a mass movement whose very numbers would wipe out the goods each individual sought for his own."[2]

The rural class historically was distinguished by land use. The land was used for the production of food, and in both Europe and Asia the farmers lived in villages and walked to their fields. This changed in the settlement of North America when farmers began to build homes on the farmland instead of living in villages and commuting to farm their land.

The three character classes have been around since the dawn of recorded history, but are too basic to describe the diversity and complexity of modern communities. Each of the three classes has been subdivided into a total of eight community character types. Types within a class may be distinguished by differences in scale, density, or design. Urban includes urban core, urban, and auto-urban. Sub-urban has been divided into suburban and estate. The rural class has three types: country-side, agriculture, and natural.

In the nineteenth century, technological advances such as the elevator, steel- and concrete-frame construction, and the automobile set in motion a series of changes that resulted in new community character types. Two of those are urban: the urban core, which was not possible without new construction technology and the elevator, and auto-urban, which was created by the automobile and with which we continue to struggle. The automobile also provides a new rural type by providing rural access, since people could live in a rural environment and commute to work in urban or sub-urban areas. The rural type of the countryside came into being as a blend of exurban residential with agricultural or natural areas.

PHYSICAL, ENVIRONMENTAL, ECONOMIC, AND SOCIAL ATTRIBUTES

Today, unlike most of the past, families have a wide range of choice in where they live. The physical elements either enable or constrain social, environmental, or economic possibilities. For example, a resident who values the social element of privacy may not choose to live in the dense urban core. It is vital to realize that the attributes change with character. For example, privacy is available only inside one's apartment in the urban core. In urban or auto-urban character types, a walled yard is essential to outdoor privacy. The sub-urban types permit increasing amounts of privacy outdoors. The physical organization of each type creates benefits or constraints for environmental, social, and economic concerns. For example, open space in sub-urban types makes it easier to protect natural resources within a new development, while natural areas protect resources by minimizing development.

Physical Attributes

There are nine design and physical attributes that are useful in describing community character types (see table 3-1).

Spatial quality is the qualitative aspect of spaces. The three

Table 3-1. Physical attributes of community character types

Character class	Urban			Sub-urban		Rural		
Character type	Urban core	Urban	Auto-urban	Suburban	Estate	Countryside	Agricultural	Natural
Spatial quality	Architectural space		Architecture, parking	Garden-like	Garden-like, natural	Pastoral	Agricultural	Natural
Spatial type	Strongly positive	Positive	Weakly positive	Negative		Infinite		
Spatial relationship	Highly enclosed	Enclosed	Weakly enclosed	Borrowed		Landscape		
Land use	Commercial	Commercial-residential		Residential-commercial	Residential	Agriculture-residential	Agricultural	Habitat
Housing type	High-rise	Mixed apartments to single-family		Single-family, attached	Single-family	Single-family	Farmstead	Cottage
Service and utilities	Full public services				Private sewer	Private rural services		
Road spacing	6 lanes @ $\frac{1}{4}$ mi.	4 lanes @ $\frac{1}{4}$ mi.		2 lanes @ $\frac{2}{3}$ mi.	2 lanes @ 4 mi.	2 lanes @ $\frac{5}{20}$ mi.		
Congestion	Very high	High		Moderate	Low	Very low	None	
Transit suitability	Very high	High	Moderate	Low	Unsuited			

classes each have different spatial qualities (physiographic environments): architectural, garden-like, and pastoral or natural.[3] Quality suggests the experience that one has in moving through the space. The garden-like setting of sub-urban types is dominated by separate homes, while pastoral or natural environments form landscapes where humans and their structures are few. Architectural space is defined or enclosed by buildings. It is a totally built environment. In auto-urban, parking competes with buildings and fills space, providing a very different experience. Garden-like space surrounds buildings, allowing them to borrow views of trees and green space. The pastoral areas are dominated by the production of food and fiber. Natural areas are habitats for plants and animals or are reserved for low-intensity recreation. At the estate level, the garden quality is often modified by landscape or rural elements like fences to lend it a more rural feel.

Spatial type is the organization of space. The three primary types are positive, negative, and infinite space. Urban spaces are positive, though they weaken from urban core to auto-urban. Suburban spaces are generally negative, while rural area spaces are infinite.

Spatial relationships are the interactions between buildings and space. For the urban types, it is usually measured by the degree of enclosure. Urban cores have very high degrees of enclosure, so much so that streets can be canyon-like. Enclosure declines from urban core to auto-urban where most space is occupied by parking. Sub-urban types borrow space for the home and community, whether these be manicured yards, parks, or natural areas. In rural character types, space expands to be a landscape, with buildings seen as trivial.

Land use is a primary tool for planning. While a full range of residential and nonresidential land uses can be built in all types, from urban core to estate, the range of uses present in a type reflects economic factors imposed by design factors. In meeting the estate character, for instance, the open space required is so large that only a very small segment of the nonresidential market would build that way. As would be expected, commercial activities are highest in urban activity centers and lowest in estate areas. Agriculture and natural habitat are the dominant land uses for the rural types, with little land being residential.

Housing type is an indicator of the average type of housing in each character type. It is a close parallel with the character type's density. High-rise apartments are unique to the urban core environment. A mix of multi-family, attached, and single-family housing is found in urban and auto-urban, and declines to mostly single-family in suburban areas. Estate and country-side housing are single-family. Farmsteads are the typical agricultural area housing. Natural areas generally should not be inhabited, but some cottages will be inevitable. Overall, the preference for single-family housing in the United States certainly has driven choices in the last sixty years.

Services and utilities describes the level and type of in-ground governmental services and utilities (e.g., water and sewer) the community character type requires. Other services, such as police, fire, and recreation, are not included here because the demand for these tends to differ by municipality rather than by character type. From urban to suburban there is a full level of public services. At the estate level, lot sizes make sewer and water very expensive to provide so there is a shift to on-site facilities. In many areas the soils permit private wells and on-site septic systems to substitute for public systems.[4] In rural areas, the citizens may be more self-reliant and demand a lower level of governmental services, such as police protection or garbage pickup. In those areas with rural water districts, estate and rural areas do not have systems that can support fire suppression because lines are too small to permit trucks to draw water from hydrants. As a result, fire protection concentrates on preventing spread rather than saving the building.

Road spacing refers to the spacing of arterial roads in relation to one another, which is critical to moving automobile traffic (particularly in metropolitan areas). The spacing of arterial roads to maintain a given level of service varies by character type. If a character type does not provide roads at the recommended spacing levels for its type, congestion is predictable.

Congestion occurs when the level of traffic on a street exceeds a certain percentage of the road's maximum capacity, leading to stop-and-go traffic and delays. Although nearly everybody complains about congestion, this is mostly subjective. Transportation engineers provide an objective measure by defining six levels of services (LOS) for roads and intersections. The top two levels (A and B) are free-flowing unless disrupted by accidents. LOS C, in which passing becomes more difficult, is often considered the ideal because it rarely experiences delays. Many communities accept LOS D, where some delay is frequent. Even when proper road spacing is provided, there is an inherent natural congestion level associated with each character type.[5] This ranges from very high in urban cores, where the intensities require large numbers of commuters, to none in the rural character types.

Transit suitability indicates the general ability of the densities of population in each of the categories to support public transit. It is at its highest in the urban core and declines until the rural, where there is no ability to support transit.

Environmental Attributes

Determining the environmental attributes of character types is more complex than with other physical characteristics (see table 3-2). Energy conservation needs and the human impact on global warming give added importance to these attributes. First, the form of development, such as the degree of clustering and level of density, can significantly shift the impact. Second, the location of development, the length of the trip to work, and the

Table 3-2. Environmental aspects of community character types

Character class	Urban			Sub-urban		Rural		
Character type	Urban core	Urban	Auto-urban	Suburban	Estate	Countryside	Agricultural	Natural
Impervious surface ratio	1.00–0.95		0.95–0.80	0.33–0.20	0.12–0.08	0.06–0.02	0.05–0.005	
On-site resource protection	None		Very little	Fair	Good	Excellent	Poor	Excellent
Storm water runoff	Very high			Moderate	Low	Very low		Minimal
Water quality per acre	Very low			Moderate	Moderately high	Moderate to high	Moderate	Very high
Water quality per person	Very high	High	Moderately high	Moderate	Moderately low	Low	Extremely low	Low
Air quality	Very low	Low		Moderate	Moderately high	High		
Heat island effect	High	Moderately high		Limited	None			

available modes of travel have major environmental effects. While the level of environmental impact is partially based on character type, there is huge potential for variation. For example, some urban cores, such as Los Angeles and Houston, have a much higher use of automobiles than Chicago or New York and thus use more energy.

Impervious surface ratio indicates the portion of land that is impervious, which means buildings or paving (see chapter 1). This is an important measure of the environmental impact for a number of resource issues. Impervious surfaces affect the ability to protect resources on the site, the amount and quality of runoff, groundwater recharge, and the heat island effect. In each case the higher the impervious surface ratio, the worse the situation is environmentally. The urban types have very high impervious surface ratios, approaching one. This falls off a great deal for sub-urban and approaches zero for the rural types.

On-site resource protection is a measure of how well resources on the specific parcel can be protected without sacrificing development potential. The rating assumes that natural resources, such as woodlands, wetlands, or floodplains, cover about 25–40 percent of the site before development. Because of the very high impervious surface ratios of urban character types, they should not develop into areas with significant resources that need to be protected. In suburban and estate, the impact on sensitive land is quite controllable with clustering (see the companion volume, *A Guide to Planning for Community Character*). Rural character types can easily avoid developing in sensitive areas, with the exception of farming, where any natural resources present are often cleared in preparing the land for agriculture.

Storm-water runoff. When rain falls on the land, most of it either runs off or soaks into the ground, ultimately reaching the water table (recharge). Runoff and groundwater recharge are inversely related. When roads, parking, or buildings are built, the amount of runoff from a storm event is increased, due to the amount of impervious surface on the site, and recharge is reduced. Increased runoff can result in environmental problems, such as pollutants flowing into streams, and can also increase the possibility of flooding. In the urban types there are only two basic choices for handling runoff. One can either pipe the water away or store it. The combined sewers (storm water and waste water) found in many cities are major sources of pollution because the flows overwhelm the treatment plants. In sub-urban areas the increased runoff can be mitigated on-site with detention using storm-water basins, which are far less costly. Rural areas generally have much less impervious surface and therefore fewer runoff problems. To the extent that storm-water flows are increased, recharge is decreased, which adversely affects groundwater supplies and low flows in streams.

Water quality per acre is the traditional way that nonpoint source pollution is measured, typically stated as a loading rate (pounds of pollutant per acre per year) running off the site. Character types have a general pollutant loading rate, based primarily on the amount of impervious surface. Some land uses are generally worse for polluted runoff, such as agriculture and golf courses (due to the chemicals that are applied). Industry has higher pollutant loadings than does commercial due to industrial chemicals washing into water systems. The per-acre basis for measuring water quality only tells the site-specific impact, important for site planning but misleading for municipal- or area-level planning.

Water quality per person. What is the best way to protect drinking water if one is building one thousand homes? The answer is nearly the complete opposite of the per-acre measure. If a hundred homes are to be built on one-acre lots, the per-acre loading rate is comparatively quite low. On the other hand, if 67 percent of the site were open space, the same hundred homes built on quarter-acre lots would result in a lower loading rate for the site and region as a whole. Thus, in planning for a municipality, one should look at the loading rate for the projected growth. The loading rate increases with density, but does so more slowly than the increase in density. Since the higher density uses less land, it also results in less pollution per person. Clustering and high densities can be used to reduce pollution potential. For nonresidential uses, auto-urban should be avoided, and urban density should be the goal in order to minimize the impact on water quality. This approach is far more sustainable than opting solely for the housing type with the lowest per-acre loading rate.

Air quality. In general the more intense the development, the worse the air quality is likely to be. This can be modified somewhat by the modal split between automobile travel and transit. The portion of heavier industries also makes a difference. While great strides have been made in the last fifty years, the air in urban areas is rarely as clean as it is in more rural areas.[6] A major reason is the more intense traffic, more heating and cooling, and the lack of tree masses that help to clean the air. Although driving greater distances is required in rural areas, the level of traffic is much lower, and areas without major industry are minor contributors to air pollution. Wooded natural areas actually help to improve air quality and sequester carbon.

Air quality is greatly affected by geography and topography. Those downwind of major pollution sources like coal-burning power plants may have far worse air quality than similar character types elsewhere in the country. Communities in valleys, such as Salt Lake City and Denver, are particularly vulnerable to periods of low air quality. Thus air quality cannot easily be generalized by type.

Heat island effect. Paved areas or other impervious surfaces such as rooftops absorb the heat of the sun during the day, which increases temperatures when the heat is radiated after the sun has gone down. This creates a higher demand for cooling energy in urban areas unless the effect is mitigated. In sub-urban areas, with their greater tree canopy, the trees will have a cooling effect in the summer and a slight warming effect in the winter (by cutting down on wind velocity). Rural areas are at ambient temperatures. Tree cover is very important here, but has limited potential in urban areas because there is no room for significant plantings. But tree planting is a mitigation strategy for all districts. Green roofs reduce the heat of roofs by as much as 50 percent and thus are very effective in urban environments.

Carbon footprint, no doubt a very important element, is not shown in the table because its relationship to character types is too complex. Carbon footprint refers to the amount of carbon that is put into the air by a person, home, or business. This measure is critical to global warming. The United States is the worst polluter because of its high energy usage. Buildings and automobiles are major emitters. A building's efficiency is determined by architectural design, and carbon-neutral buildings can be designed for all character types. Travel by automobile increases as one goes from urban to sub-urban types. More energy-efficient transit requires urban densities in order to be feasible. But the heat island is an urban problem. The landscaping and borrowed space in sub-urban types promotes more efficient heating and cooling. Clustering in suburban and estate character types can increase density and preserve wetlands and woodlands, which are carbon sinks, reducing carbon footprints. These contrasting values make rating impossible. The last chapter in the companion book, *A Guide to Planning for Community Character,* includes a discussion of applying community character to make communities more sustainable and reduce their carbon footprint.

Social and Economic Attributes

There are nine economic and social attributes that relate to each of the community character types (see table 3-3). Caution is needed here, as some social and economic attributes are clearly more powerfully related to the scale of the community rather than character type. For example, the economic function of urban areas will vary with the scale of the community.

Function is an economic and social indicator of the general activity of the community character type. The categories used are: intensive activity, activity center, residential retreat, exurban, food and fiber, and wild. Urban types evolved as activity centers that allowed specialization, meaning the manufacture, sale, and trade in goods other than food. All urban types are the centers of these activities. Urban cores relate to the sector-scale areas and thus have a much higher level of intensity. Sub-urban

Table 3-3. Social and economic attributes of community character types

Character class	Urban			Sub-urban		Rural		
Character type	Urban core	Urban	Auto-urban	Suburban	Estate	Countryside	Agricultural	Natural
Function	Intensive activity	Activity center		Residential retreat		Exurban	Food and fiber	Wild
Economic role	Regional CBD	CBD subregion to community		Community CBD	Convenience	Agricultural		Protect environment, tourism, recreation
Workforce	Major importer	Importer		Exporter		Exporter	Internal	
Encounter level	Very high	High	Weakly high	Moderate	Moderately low	Low	Rare	
Site of social contact	Streets/public space			Yards/parks	Yards/home	Events		
Privacy	In home	In home/courtyards		Home/yards	Yards/home	Yards/home	Pervasive	
Child play	Street/public spaces			Yards/public spaces		Yards/open	Open	
Opportunities for relaxation	Activities/vacation away	Home at night/weekends				Surrounding open land or groups		
Safety from crime	Low		Moderately low	Moderate	Moderately high	High	Very high	

types were family-oriented places of residential living designed to provide escape from the activity centers. Countryside is similar to sub-urban, but more remote. In the past, its remoteness discouraged development because travel to the city for work was too difficult. The growing of food and fiber was the purpose of rural communities. Wild describes the natural areas, on which there were originally no permanent settlements and human activity was limited to hunting and gathering, which now serve as habitat preserves.

Economic role differs from function in that it addresses the economic activity that can be found in community character types. It reflects the fact that at any scale beyond neighborhood there will be some form of economic activity. The urban and auto-urban roles are totally linked to the community scale. The sub-urban types are economically limited due to the maximum density that can be achieved while maintaining their character. The rural types' economic role is little different than their function with the exception of the natural type, where parks and tourism have introduced economic activity.

Workforce addresses the relationship of home to place of work, and how this affects character. For example, urban areas are generally importers of workers. This is most dramatic in the urban core, which generally experiences a large influx of workers during the day and an exodus of workers in the evening. Sub-urban communities typically export workers. As jobs move out of cities to the suburbs, there has become a more balanced commute, with residents of suburbs commuting to cities and city residents commuting to jobs in auto-urban areas in the suburbs. When suburbs successfully attract businesses, the auto-urban areas that house the business confuse whether a suburb is auto-urban or suburban, which warrants the negative name "slurb" (see chapter 1). Edge cities also have a mix of auto-urban commercial and urban core offices and hotels. These urban character types bring with them congestion levels that disrupt the quiet, low-traffic streets that are essential for a family retreat. Agricultural and natural areas are generally in balance, with residents working the land they live on, while the countryside has almost no employment, so its workers commute to cities or suburbs.

Encounter level measures the opportunity (from rare to extremely high) to encounter people or business, shopping, social, or cultural opportunities within short distances and travel time. A study of the history of urban places indicates that high encounter levels are essential to commerce, social, and cultural activities. As a value, the desire for different levels of encounter is often sensitive to life-cycle changes. Young, single people and empty nesters are more likely to want high encounter levels, which are found in urban areas. At rural densities, homes are so far separated that even neighboring requires intent, and in natural areas even seeing a person is rare.

Site of social contact addresses the space where social contact occurs in a community. It is closely related to the encounter level, as the design of a community can encourage or discourage encounters. In urban areas, public spaces such as the sidewalk, park, or plaza, or private buildings, restaurants, bars, and so forth are where people meet to socialize. In sub-urban classes, socializing in yards and homes becomes very important because of the focus on family and children. Parks are also important, particularly in the sub-urban and urban types. In rural types, social activities are usually planned group events (religious or festivals) or meetings at key locations, such as the post office or agricultural service uses (where people meet while getting essential supplies).

Privacy is an essential human need. Both individuals and families need opportunities for privacy. How and where privacy can be provided is an important distinction between character types. In the urban core and much of urban or auto-urban multi-family, it can only be provided indoors. In single-family urban or auto-urban, privacy will be either indoors or in walled outdoor rooms (courtyards or patios). Sub-urban class communities use yards to provide outdoor privacy in addition to indoor spaces. In rural areas, homes are so remote from one another that privacy ceases to become an issue; in fact, isolation can become a problem for some people.

Child play. Where children can safely play represents another social concern. In most urban areas, streets, alleys, sidewalks, and public spaces (parks, playgrounds, and institutional spaces such as schools) provide areas for children's recreation. Whether all these areas are safe is a question that led a great number of families over the past fifty years to move to suburban areas, where it was perceived that the yards of the family and the neighbors were far safer than streets and alleys. Estate areas are similarly perceived as safe, but distances reduce playing opportunities. Public spaces, particularly parks and schools, continue to provide recreation opportunities in both sub-urban types. In rural areas, children still tend to roam at will from yards to the rural landscape. But this is an issue undergoing change. In both city and suburb, the conventional wisdom was that one adult was around to view the proceedings in the street or yard. This is rarely true today, because children are packed off to organized and supervised activities. This may weaken the appeal of suburbs, as the yard is not used as frequently but still demands maintenance. For both urban and sub-urban areas, an important question is whether there is adequate recreation land.

Opportunities for relaxation. When the stress of one's workplace or living environment builds up, there is need for relief. In the urban types, a variety of social, sporting events, and cultural activities are the primary relief from both home and work. For another subset of the urban population, a weekend getaway or vacation is needed to provide the release. The suburb was originally a nightly escape for the worker, whose family was spared the stress of an intense urban environment. The care of the yard was therapy as well as an opportunity for family-oriented activities. Rural areas reverse the roles, with the residents traveling to the city to find excitement. The two-income household is changing the types of opportunities available in all areas. The dedication of children to sports or other activities cuts into visits or vacations to natural areas and regional, state, or national parks. This is a changing dynamic that may well alter the current mix of types.

Safety from crime is a measure of security. Historically, the city provided safety from invasion behind walls. The residents of suburbs or rural areas fled to the cities if they had the opportunity. The crime in cities is now viewed as a greater threat than crime in other character classes. While some of this is anecdotal, in small towns and more sub-urban and rural areas there is less concern and people routinely leave their cars or even houses unlocked.

The values associated with different character classes and types can affect where one may choose to live. Planners, architects, and New Urbanists often seek to encourage a particular character type, but this will fail if the type does not match what people desire. In planning larger communities, flexibility by the planners is important. Obviously, one does not want people to be forced out of the municipality because their preferred community character type is not permitted by the zoning; in such a situation, they will simply relocate elsewhere in the area.

URBAN CLASS

Until the twentieth century there was only the urban type within this class; urban core and auto-urban are new types. All three share some important characteristics that distinguish the urban from sub-urban or rural classes. All urban types mix retail, employment, cultural institutions, and living environments. The intensity of uses and high encounter levels make the urban class favorable to business. All three types share these characteristics to different degrees, with urban cores having the greatest concentration and largest market. The result of good urban design applied to any type is an urban community that is successful in concentrating large numbers of people and potential transaction opportunities in small areas.

While the words normally carry a negative connotation, "congestion" and "crowds" convey the types of human interactions that mark the successful urban place. Retailers live for the peak shopping days, a crowd, represents a high encounter level, indicating success. High encounter levels in this instance refer both to people-to-people and people-to-service contacts. While customers may complain about fighting the crowds, they would be suspicious of a retail area that was not crowded. The same is true of areas that offer social and cultural opportunities. The successful commercial areas have magnets that draw customers into districts, be it a street with department stores, a regional mall, or the bazaar of the Middle East. The urban types vary in how this is accomplished. The urban core differs from the urban most visibly by its high-rise buildings and canyon-like streets, which permit an extreme concentration of people and businesses. Auto-urban spreads out the urban uses with roads and parking areas that are far more extensive than the buildings they serve.

The structuring of the activity centers is a critical element of the urban types, and it influences the design of buildings and spaces. The architectural character of urban spaces was a clear response to the needs of urban areas to encourage maximum encounters. The relationship of buildings to open areas that served as activity centers left little private or discretionary space for residents. This form of design permitted maximum access for different activities to either the street or the squares. The result was that the ratio of building mass to the total ground area of the urban community had to be high to create enclosure. This is seen in a drawing type called the figure-ground (see chapter 1). In figure 3-1, the black represents building coverage and the white the streets, sidewalks, squares, or other spaces not occupied by buildings. The spaces were created as areas absent buildings and can be called positive space because of the enclosing presence of the buildings. The degree of enclosure is one of the key variables among the three types of urban communities, with urban cores having the greatest enclosure and auto-urban the least.

Urban environments are almost exclusively man-made. While some urban areas have enough parks, many more do not,

Figure 3-1. Figure-ground drawing for urban street.

Figure 3-2. Urban neighborhood. Chicago, Illinois.

Figure 3-3. Urban core. Chicago, Illinois.

Figure 3-4. Auto-urban: more space occupied by parking than buildings. Northbrook, Illinois.

and the parks that do exist have significant areas of pavement. Only where physical features preclude building is the natural environment left even partially intact; wetlands and shorelines have been routinely filled, and even steep, unstable slopes have been built on.[7] The high value of the land for use as activity centers creates the economic power to build in otherwise-marginal areas. The high intensities of use require that the communities provide full service, with public water, sewer, roads, and maximum levels of police, fire, and other governmental services.

Urban Types

Urban settlements evolved over several thousand years with a relatively common set of design principles. While cultural and temporal variations exist, the urban place as an architecturally dominated environment with building-enclosed space is remarkably consistent. Figure 3-2 provides an aerial view of an urban portion of the city of Chicago. Urban communities have spaces with high degrees of enclosure as measured by D/H (see chapter 1) when the width of streets, squares, or plazas is divided by the height of surrounding buildings. For most of history, the technology of building construction limited the practical height of buildings, so these spaces varied within a fairly narrow range. They succeed primarily as pedestrian environments.

With the addition of efficient vertical transportation, modern structural technologies, and the automobile, two new urban types evolved: the urban core and auto-urban. The central business districts of large cities exhibit the urban core character (as indicated in figure 3-3), which is characterized by the dominance of high-rise buildings. The building height means that floor area ratios greater than ten are easily possible, though in most urban areas it is less than two.

Since the first towns appeared, urban places were predominantly pedestrian. While the Industrial Revolution introduced the streetcar and passenger rail, most people still walked at either end of the line. Those modes of transit increased concentration in the retail and employment centers, but the neighborhoods changed little. The automobile, however, changed everything. It consumed land that was previously devoted to buildings. Densities were lowered due to the change in land allocation and the ability to travel greater distances quickly. Since the majority of the great urban spaces were conceived primarily for pedestrians, the introduction of the automobile strained the architectural design.[8] Like it or not, the automobile has brought a new urban form into existence—auto-urban—where parking and streets consume a greater percentage of land than do commercial or office land uses (see figure 3-4).

In describing the varying types, urban is addressed first because it is the original urban type from which the others have evolved. Urban remains a valid design type, and all urban spaces are positive and generally enclosing. As introduced in chapter 1, the concept of enclosure can be measured using the distance/height ratio (D/H), which is the distance across a space divided by the height of the surrounding buildings. Building coverage—the area covered by buildings divided by the site area—and figure-ground drawings all also shed light on this issue.

The relationship of the surrounding buildings to a particular space is quantified by D/H (see figure 3-5). The Mykonos pedestrian street's D/H is approximately 0.3, with the street being one-third the building height. The square in figure 3-6 has a D/H of about 1.0, which allows for both circulation and outdoor activities. When D/H exceeds 5.0, enclosure is lost; figure 3-7 shows a parking area that can fill with automobiles, creating a very unfriendly space. Most architectural commentators indicate that D/H in an urban space should not exceed 4 or 5. A space that is too large in comparison to its surrounding buildings loses its identity and ability to focus activities. Further, even if a plan view of a space seems to show enclosure, it will not be identified visually. A failure to achieve visual enclosure means a loss of the essential quality of the urban space, while too much enclosure can become oppressive. The total size and degree of enclosure can help determine the suitability of the space for activities, from formal or ritualistic to intimate. The classic urban space also had well-defined building coverage ratios.

Urban

A strongly enclosed environment characterizes the urban type. Streets typically have D/H values ranging from less than one to

Figure 3-5. Enclosure: D/H = 0.3. Mykonos, Greece.

Figure 3-6. Enclosure: D/H = 1.0. Tübingen, Germany.

Figure 3-7. Lack of enclosure: D/H = 8.0. Mundelein, Illinois.

Figure 3.8. Pedestrian precinct. Carmel, California.

about two. Squares or other spaces should not exceed four. Some narrow streets or pedestrian ways may have D/Hs as low as 0.25. All urban environments also exhibit a human scale. There are a number of techniques that are useful for thinking about human scale (see chapter 1). The one-story pedestrian precinct shown in figure 3-8 clearly has a human scale, with buildings no more than a few times the height of a human and broken into elements that are rarely larger than two human-scale units. The human-scale unit can be used to define spatial ranges for different purposes, from intimate spaces to public spaces. It may also be used with social scales that relate the space to its function. It sets an upper limit on the average height of buildings at five to six stories. Taller buildings require a base that strongly relates to the human scale; since pedestrians cannot easily see the higher parts without looking up, there needs to be three distinct elements to the building: base, body, and top or cap.

Landscaping, in terms of vegetation, is an optional feature in urban design. There are great urban spaces with no trees or other vegetative masses; the pavement, public art, fountains, street furniture, and buildings are all the designer needs to produce a dynamic space. Urban residential areas do benefit aesthetically from street trees, as well as for their role in reducing the heat island effect and slowing runoff. When used in sufficient quantities, street and yard trees can alter the character of an area; when they are taller than the homes, they shelter the dwellings and decrease the sense of enclosure. It should also be noted that in community-preference exercises, examples with significant trees often receive the highest approval ratings.[9] In urban residential areas, landscaping becomes more important because of its aesthetic and environmental values.

Urban design will flourish only when structured parking is combined with mixed uses. Without structured parking, surface parking converts an area to auto-urban in character by pushing D/H to greater than five. Mixed uses provide additional housing and office space above retail to make activity centers more intense, providing on-site customers. The mixed use can in many cases reduce parking requirements because uses with different peak-parking needs can get double use out of some spaces. Most important, the mixed use makes possible higher intensities so that urban environments use less land.

Mixed use may result in a decrease in people using cars to get to some uses. But caution is needed—some communities are mandating mixed-use structures and ground-floor retail. This is unwise since there is not always a market for this space and it can sit empty.[10]

Having adjoining urban residential is a better strategy than forcing each building into a fixed mode. This creates a larger market of households without spreading out the commercial. The goal of urban commercial areas is to make walking and shopping as pleasurable as possible so that pedestrians spend more time and money there.

Visual pleasure can be created by interesting buildings, street furniture, pavement, street art, plantings, attractive signs, and changes in elevation. The importance of this type of good design cannot be overemphasized. These can make the difference between a poor- and high-quality urban place. Some degree of physical comfort is needed, particularly for the very young and the elderly, for whom places to sit are important elements. Figure 3-9 illustrates a street in Chapel Hill, North Carolina, whose sidewalk is wide enough to provide for both pedestrians and commercial activity. Boston's Faneuil Hall marketplace (see figure 3-10) illustrates a successful pedestrian precinct. Historically, conflict between modes of travel within urban spaces was generally low as most traffic was pedestrian.[11] With the sharing of streets by people and cars, retention of a pleasing pedestrian precinct is a critical element of urban design.

Figure 3.9. Street vendor creates activity. Chapel Hill, North Carolina.

Figure 3.10. Pedestrian plaza. Boston, Massachusetts.

Urban Core

The urban core was made possible by the advent of iron and steel construction and elevators that permitted the creation of the skyscraper. Once buildings were free to increase in height, the degree of enclosure was dramatically altered and the buildings grew to an inhuman scale. In some cases a single building occupies an entire block, a complete change from the human scale of buildings with twenty to fifty feet of street frontage.

Skyscrapers dwarf humans. At sixty feet (four to five stories), a building is ten times the height of a human; when a building reaches twenty stories, it is more than forty-four times

Figure 3-11. Urban core enclosure. Chicago, Illinois.

Figure 3-12. Boston Common a large urban core open space. Boston, Massachusetts.

human height. At this level it is necessary to tilt one's head back to see the skyline across the street; architects compensate for this by creating a compelling base architecture so that people focus on the base, not the rest of the building. The tall building means that we see the skyline only of buildings more than a block away, instead of those across the street. The building top is an important element of the design, yet at the inhuman scale this aspect of the building is rarely seen at street level. As the length of the base at street level increases, one loses the ability to recognize a friend at the other end of the building. This impersonal or event scale leaves people feeling a connection only with the things in the immediate vicinity, losing a sense of space and buildings as a whole. The D/H of an eighty-foot-wide street and twenty-story building falls below 0.3. A space fifteen feet wide provides the same D/H with a four-story building. The D/H and change in scale creates a very different spatial character, and the buildings in urban cores may often average forty or more stories. Figure 3-11 illustrates the inhuman scale, where the theater sign is eight stories high and the tops of buildings over two blocks away require one to look up. In urban cores, a space the size of a football field barely exceeds a D/H of one.

Taller buildings dramatically alter the degree to which light penetrates to the streets, so that there is only a narrow window of time when one can walk down the sunny side of a street. The shade also makes the street less inviting, except in the hottest of climates. Architects must compensate for the impact of the change in scale for the pedestrian. Louis Sullivan and other early architects of skyscrapers looked at buildings as having a base, middle, and cap or top, and made these three elements read visually. This enabled the base (one or two stories) to be designed to promote a relationship to pedestrians, and let the middle of the building be a less-dominant shaft that led the eye up to the cap at the skyline. This design strategy is intended to mitigate scale, but the problem is that when all the buildings are of this scale, it is hard to find a place where one is far enough away to take this in without moving one's head to see it.

The urban core also affects open spaces such as parks. Savannah, Georgia's marvelous parks are about the size of a block. Urban core parks like Boston Common (see figure 3-12) and Central Park in New York are much larger and should be considered models. New Zealand cities, such as Christchurch and Auckland, are notable for having large-scale parks in or abutting their urban cores. Cities like Chicago, on the other hand, capitalize on their waterfronts.

While architects responded visually to the change of scale in the facades of the buildings, urban cores were simply built on top of an older urban street pattern. Planners and architects alike failed to question whether the street pattern of an urban community was appropriate for an urban core. Forcing pedestrians to share the street with roads six or eight lanes wide makes little sense. There is a better model for urban cores than an urban grid system. A grade-separated pedestrian precinct, with the pedestrian level above the automobile street, is the most desirable structure for urban cores (see the companion book, *A Guide to Planning for Community Character*, for further discussion). There is no reason that a person should not be able to freely cross a pedestrian precinct on a whim without having to be controlled by traffic lights. A pedestrian precinct at-grade forces the pedestrian to compete with automobiles and trucks. By placing the pedestrian precinct on a separate level from car and truck traffic the conflict is removed. One is then free to design the pedestrian area for pedestrian activities, instead of squeezing it on the sides of vehicular streets; in fact, it may run through buildings as well as around them. Spaces for eating, sitting, or meeting can be designed into such a precinct.

Urban cores are largely office with ground-floor commercial, with only occasional residential units (usually older buildings on the fringe). All too often the existing urban cores are nearly abandoned at night when the office workers go home. A more balanced mix of land uses resulting in a twenty-four-hour city is desirable. Urban cores are best when served by a well-developed transit system because the very high intensities congest the streets. London's success with congestion pricing, which charges for auto access to the urban core, indicates that these areas can be designed with transit or people movers that greatly reduce the need for automobiles.

Auto-Urban

Auto-urban evolved in response to the need to park automobiles, rather than as the result of planning. The ability to park in front of a use greatly influenced the way retail and service businesses operate. A common auto-urban feature is strip development, generally commercial in nature, along an arterial or collector street. This is not a sub-urban form; the cities in the late nineteenth and early twentieth centuries had commercial uses located on major arterial streets with streetcar service, creating the first strips.[12] Commercial is naturally attracted to corridors that move a large volume of people.

Auto-urban environments are characterized by land where automobiles, parking, and roads consume more land than do buildings. The building masses differ from traditional urban areas by largely being one-story, often-freestanding uses surrounded by a sea of parking. The combination of streets and at-grade, surface parking lots totally alters the character of the auto-urban environment by reducing building coverage, creating spaces devoted to parking cars, and lowering the intensity of use. The figure-ground pattern of an auto-urban street is very different from that of the traditional urban street that evolved from 1850 to 1940. The extent of parking and streets serves to separate land uses, and results in an increase in the D/H value to six or more, greatly weakening enclosure. Using taller buildings is not effective because it decreases building coverage and increases the proportion of an area covered by parking.

What the automobile has done in auto-urban is to create sprawl by using far more land than an urban community containing the same land uses. The classic urban community had between 10 and perhaps 20 percent of its area devoted to circulation in the form of streets and plazas, thus ensuring enclosure. In auto-urban the streets and parking consume 60 percent or more of the land.

A second problem in auto-urban areas is that the pedestrian precinct has effectively been lost. The large amount of land consumed for parking cars and moving traffic forces the wide separation of buildings, which lengthens walking time. Often this means that each building is almost totally isolated by parking. The increase in the size of stores, culminating in the big box, further decreases pedestrian accessibility. In the strip, the parking and major road effectively prohibit pedestrian access to uses across the street, as can be seen in figure 3-13. In regional malls, the sea of parking is so large as to totally discourage walking across the parking lot to outparcel restaurants or other uses.

Not only is pedestrian access limited, but automobile access is poorly linked, forcing even short automobile trips from one use to another to use arterials or collectors, which increases congestion. But that does not mean pedestrian precincts are impossible in auto-urban areas. Figure 3-14 illustrates a strip mall where an effort has been made to create a pedestrian precinct that is more than a sidewalk.

The availability of cheaper land allows office or industrial park developers to surround their buildings with lawns, again increasing building separation. The result is the combination of lawns and large parking areas that again result in a loss of enclosure and increased walking distances. The green space is not adequate to create a suburban character.

The aesthetics of auto-urban are often terrible. Highways lined by individual buildings and small strip centers (three to six stores) are the worst because the businesses do not attempt to create a place; they are often more interested in the size of their signs, paying no attention to the impact on their neighbors or the public. Signs, corporate architecture, and a lack of landscaping combine to make many auto-urban areas unattractive. Larger, modern shopping centers pay more attention to design, creating a streetscape with varied setbacks, landscaping, seating, and lighting adjoining the parking. Thus design can make substantial improvements. The handling of the large areas of parking that customers ultimately must traverse, however, is the one factor that design cannot eliminate.

The auto-urban environment serves the same function as do urban and urban core environments: they are centers of activity. Businesses concentrate in order to reinforce one another and provide a positive marketing tool; they want high levels of exposure to potential customers. Like their urban counterparts, they seek to locate on roads with high volumes of traffic. The difference is that customers nearly all come by automobile. For a great many of these uses the market area is so large that most customers could not walk there, no matter how attractive the experience. Likewise, the amount or size of the purchases also works against pedestrian shopping.

The evolution of commercial areas has lead to outparcels on the road frontage being sold off to small users: gas stations, food service, banks, and some forms of retail. Residential and industrial uses also moved to auto-urban contexts. The apartment

Figure 3-13. Auto-urban. Edinburg, Texas.

Figure 3-14. Auto-urban pedestrian space. Boca Raton, Florida.

building and townhouse development have all taken on an auto-urban character. As development moved out, these housing types were clustered around parking fields rather than oriented toward streets and parks. Industrial uses moved out of multi-story, urban loft buildings into one-story facilities. The logical task facing the planning profession is not how to make all these uses revert to an old model, but rather to develop a framework for design of these areas that promotes a better environment, true pedestrian activity, and a better circulation system (see the companion book, *A Guide to Planning for Community Character*, for further discussion).

While there are some differences between commercial, service, office, and industry, they share very similar problems. While industry does not require the parking of the other uses, the truck loading areas create the same lack of enclosure. Residential, on the other hand, is very different. The automobile does not take up the majority of the land. The dividing line between urban and auto-urban residential is far more subtle, as will be discussed in greater detail in the second book. The distinction is primarily how parking is dealt with. Urban single-family and attached single-family have parking in the rear, accessed from an alley. Front-load garages or parking lots in front of the homes all indicate auto-urban. Multi-family housing with access from parking lots will nearly always be auto-urban unless there is structured parking. Is parking what you see from the street or access area? If so, the area will most likely be auto-urban rather than urban.

The quality of auto-urban commercial has improved in recent years. More communities are forcing better architecture, signage, and landscaping. Mandating commercial buildings be built to the sidewalk line does not make for an urban environment, however, because with at-grade parking most customers must still cross large parking lots to reach stores, just like at malls. With surface parking, making a taller building increases the percent of the site devoted to parking because the additional floor area requires yet more parking. With four-story buildings, nearly 90 percent of the area would be devoted to surface parking. Thus only where government is confident enough to mandate structured parking will it be possible to create the enclosure essential to urban design. Structured parking means that building masses can again cover 80–90 percent of the site, as shown in the figure-ground drawing (figure 3-1). A street with buildings on the sidewalk line surrounded by parking is no different than a mall surrounded by parking. Many cities now require parking structures to be attractive and have ground-level shops, or perimeter offices to camouflage the use. Thus more attention is still required to improve auto-urban design.

SUB-URBAN CLASS

The term "suburban" is unfortunately both a geographic and character term. This book uses "suburb" or "suburbia" to denote the geographic intent. Sub-urban refers to the class, while suburban is a type. There was a time when city and suburb could clearly be described, so that both geographical location and character would be clearly understood.

As introduced in chapter 1, the term "sub-urban" means less than urban, or perhaps more accurately, not urban. A major shift in spatial relationships differentiates sub-urban from urban character types. In moving out of the city, it was possible to design living environments in a more spacious manner. Sub-urban types are based on a shift to a different, nonurban, spatial relationship between buildings and space. Sub-urban space is negative or borrowed space, differentiating it from urban space, which is positive or enclosed. Its character is a garden-like quality, in contrast to architectural space. While suburbs contain many buildings, architectural enclosure is undesirable because open space creates the desired natural character. This garden quality, in which the trees arch over and shelter streets and dwellings, is the visual ideal, as seen in figure 3-15. In sub-urban environments there are two competing masses or volumes: buildings and trees (landscaping). The landscape is dominant and is what leads to the garden-like quality. Lewis Mumford notes that Leon Battista Alberti's idealized description of the suburb from 1485 "might also stand as the classic last word" on the subject: "The great beauties of such a retreat are being near the city, upon an open airy road, and on a pleasant spot of ground. . . . Nor should there be any want of pleasant landscapes, flowery mead, open champains, shady groves or limpid brooks, or streams and lakes for swimming."[13]

Figure 3-15. Suburban: garden-like space with large trees. Sherman, Texas.

The lack of enclosure, the garden-like quality, and the borrowed space are critical to this sub-urban character. To achieve the difference between an urban, single-family dwelling and a suburban one, there are two approaches to providing the needed borrowed space. The simple approach is to increase the lot size so that borrowed space is available in the form of a large yard on each individual lot. The other approach is clustering—the organization of buildings and open spaces so that views from each building are directed to the open space rather than to the adjoining buildings—which represents a better alternative. The lots are smaller, even similar in size to urban single-family, but the reduction of lot size is used to create borrowed space that is commonly owned. Enlarging lots so that each home is surrounded by borrowed space constrains the achievable density; with clustering, buildings share views of borrowed open space. A second problem with the large-lot approach is that it is less sustainable and more destructive of the environment.

Sub-urban areas were always different from a land use perspective. Historically, they were predominantly residential. The sub-urban lifestyle was an escape from the activities of the city, a quieter place to raise a family. A sub-urban yard has a multitude of uses—as an outdoor living room, entertainment area, eating area, or recreation area—and offers privacy or semi-privacy outdoors. The yard was often seen as therapeutic, its maintenance being a relief compared to the stress of work. Borrowed space expands one's views into landscapes not found in urban settings.

It seems counterintuitive that bringing buildings closer together provides more spaciousness. In the first row of figure 3-16, very high percentages of green space (95 or 98.5 percent) are shown. While pervasive, the space is not organized. The thirty buildings shown constitute a rather uniform environment that is similar in every direction. Simply by pairing the units in the 95 percent example, spaces are created that are more recognizable and provide a structure to the environment (the second row of figure 3-16). The reason for this is that the building masses are more compact and spaces are increased, because there are now fifteen groupings rather than thirty individual buildings. More views to the horizon are opened up. If the clustering is continued so that there are three clusters in the bottom row, the spaces become stronger and more dominant. Most sub-

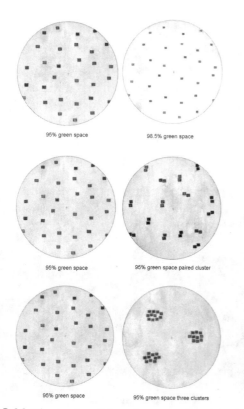

95% green space

98.5% green space

95% green space

95% green space paired cluster

95% green space

95% green space three clusters

Figure 3-16. The paradox of clustering: more clustering creates a greater sense of space.

urbs have lots of borrowed open space initially, since the surrounding land is undeveloped. As the suburb matures the open space disappears, and in many cases the residents become dissatisfied with the character as the last open space is developed. Cluster developments provide common open space for the entire community. Randall Arendt's *Rural by Design* contains some thirty-nine examples of clustering (both residential and mixed use).[14]

Landscaping is critical to either approach to borrowed open space. One might simply call it camouflage, but that would be too simple. Building volumes create space through enclosure. Trees can create volume, screens, and even a sense of enclosure, as can hedges. Trees represent a green volume that can be manipulated by the designer. Sub-urban environments require a green volume to balance and cancel the building volumes. In figure 3-17 masses of trees are set into the 95 percent green space. A vegetative mass creates a sense of space because it simultaneously screens some buildings from view and creates a different volume that interrupts the horizon. In mature suburban areas the trees arch over streets and buildings alike, seeming to enclose the entire area.

Figures 3-18a and 3-18b are a typical pair of pictures used in community preference surveys. The first shows the newly constructed suburban homes with only a few immature plantings. The second shows urban houses on a tree-lined street where some of the trees are sixty years old. The majority of people prefer the urban house with the trees to the new home with none, even though the new home has a larger lot. This

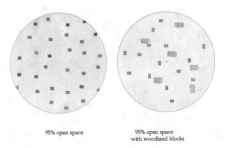

95% open space   95% open space
with woodland blocks

Figure 3-17. Artificial horizon hides development.

Figure 3-18a. New suburban with immature trees. Vernon Hills, Illinois.

Figure 3-18b. Mature urban with sixty-year-old trees. Franklin, Tennessee.

Figure 3-19a. One-acre wooded lot. McHenry County, Illinois.

Figure 3-19b. One-acre lot with a few twenty-year-old trees. Chesterfield, Missouri.

type of survey, promoted by the New Urbanists, is essentially dishonest because vegetation and character are both varied. The trees are critical to character and quality. It is important to seek to limit the variables so that the deciding factor is either character or landscaping.

Figures 3-19a and 3-19b each show homes in one-acre zoning districts, with both close to the same age and trees make the difference. The home on the left has preserved trees, taller than the house and sheltering it, while the lot on the right is mostly open lawn. It is the vegetation that creates the desired image. The preference for a mature, landscaped lot is consistent in both urban and sub-urban environments; and in Niesson's book[15] on community preference surveys, pictures with significant green volumes are usually given the highest ratings.

The majority of borrowed space in today's suburbs is not designed space but undeveloped land. While the adjoining farmland is often an important quality to sub-urban residents and clearly defines their environment, experience should tell us that it will eventually be developed. If the open space provides a critical component of the suburbs' character, then preserving some of it is essential. When initial subdivisions are surrounded by undeveloped farmland, the size of the lot is of little importance because the homeowners have borrowed views over the undeveloped land. Development of the borrowed space will reach a critical point at which the community transitions toward a more urban character. If the mature suburb has preserved sufficient open space, the sub-urban character will be maintained.

Eventually, citizens become concerned with the loss of open space and turn out to oppose the development of the neighboring farm (see figure 3-20), which often has lots of the same size as the established developments. These activists are referred to as NIMBYs or CAVE people.[16] Unfortunately, the NIMBYs' own subdivision destroyed a piece of the community's character, just as the farm proposed for development will destroy another piece. Community character identifies the importance of open space to a sub-urban community and provides clustering as a means of preserving that character; that way, when the community is fully developed, there will still be adequate borrowed space.

The term "borrowed space" has been selected not only to define its functional value of permitting buildings to borrow views across open land, but also to recognize the unfortunate practice of using other peoples' land as open space to create character. Clustering to preserve open space is easily accomplished with proper planning and zoning. The alternative to clustering requires buying adequate park land. In the beginning of a suburb's development, there is plenty of cheap land and the community cannot see the need to raise taxes to buy parks. When the need becomes critical, however, the land has dramatically appreciated and the result all too often is communities with inadequate open space that have lost their character. The need for open space has not been communicated to the public in comprehensive plans. Thus in only a few communities is preservation of open space a key element in planning and zoning.[17]

The garden-like quality of sub-urban space is also a result of space being an extension of the buildings' views out to the surrounding lot. There are three elements that contribute to this: street trees, on-lot landscaping, and open space. Figure 3-21 illustrates the ideal of trees arching over the street and sheltering both the street and homes. On-lot landscaping permits the homeowner to arrange the views from windows to create private borrowed space and recreation areas for sitting, playing, or entertaining. Figure 3-22 illustrates the sheltering of the house and how the trees reduce the building's scale. Open space provides the individual dwelling unit more distant borrowed space and serves as an element for the community at the cluster/block and neighborhood scales. The open space can be a formal structured element (a park or green; see figure 3-23), or more organic

Figure 3-20. Borrowed open space: undeveloped land. Lake County, Illinois.

Figure 3-21. Trees arch over street and homes. Savannah, Georgia.

Figure 3-22. Trees shelter home. Orange County, North Carolina.

Figure 3-23. Park provides borrowed open space. Wauseon, Ohio.

Figure 3-24. Borrowed open space in cluster development. Crystal Lake, Illinois.

in its form, particularly natural space (see figure 3-24). In some areas, simply preserving existing vegetation is sufficient. More often, however, the planner will have to provide open space and landscaping to create the sheltering tree canopy and borrowed spaces that are part of every development.

Another way to view the space issue is through the relationship between buildings and landscape. This relationship can be measured with building volumes and landscape volumes. The suburbs evolved away from the city with much more spacious lots, resulting in a balance between green landscape volumes and building volumes in which the landscape volume is dominant. This is a mathematical way to explain the results of community preference surveys favoring sites with mature landscaping.

In sub-urban areas the pedestrian precinct, so essential to urban character, is transformed. While pedestrian activity is frequent, bicycle, skateboard, or in-line skates, are modes used particularly by children. Yards replace the street and sidewalk for play activities, moving from public space to private space. Instead of an enclosed precinct of streets, sub-urban communities provide a mix of yards, open space, and streets that constitute the majority of the land; while sidewalks or trails are important, a pedestrian precinct is no longer a viable concept.

Sub-urban functions and design character evolved in the older suburbs, which were largely bedroom communities. Because the suburb was principally a residential area, it had no need for the high levels of interaction that characterize urban settlements. In fact, the lower levels of encounter ratios provided the very qualities that were sought out for a place to raise a family. Personal relationships and neighboring are interactions on a person-to-person basis and represent a strong attraction of sub-urban living. In early rail suburbs the communities had urban centers, with surrounding residential areas all having a sub-urban character. That urban center provided community-scale goods and services, but the majority of residents commuted to the city for employment. The term "bedroom suburb" was appropriate and the family orientation reflected that. That has changed dramatically in metropolitan areas; the road network opened whole counties to development, and regional commercial and employment moved to the suburbs. Both of those uses required an urban character type. As a result, the suburbs contain a mix of urban, auto-urban, suburban, and estate character. The arterial roads are mostly lined with auto-urban uses, so it is an error to talk about suburbs as suburban in character. If fact, most suburbs have a confused character.

Community character provides the tools to make choices. It is possible to design retail, office, or industrial uses to have a suburban character, but they require open space ratios of 50–70 percent. That open space is expensive, and the encounter levels are relatively low. This alters the economics of these uses; they can be built as urban, but then the community must seek a balance of the types that yield the desired overall character. In chapter 5 a community character triangle is discussed that assists in selecting the desired mix of character types.

Unlike the urban environments, the two levels of sub-urban settlement do not have unique structural characteristics that require different design criteria. The terms "suburban" and "estate" have been selected to divide the sub-urban character area into two useful classifications for development in today's suburbs. The difference is primarily one of intensity and utility services.

Suburban

This classification accommodates the modern suburb that has been made possible by rail and automobiles. It is the higher density of the two suburban types, generally ranging from about one to three dwelling units per acre. The lower end of density is achieved with large-lot, single-family housing. The higher intensities are achieved with clustered development and accompanying open space. Suburban densities require public sewer and water. The vacant land sketched in figure 3-25 is initially borrowed and then lost to development. The residents borrow the views that make the area seem rural. The loss of borrowed space creeps up on communities. A new suburb will be 50 percent open (undeveloped) for roughly half its life. Only when development begins to chew up the remaining 30–40 percent do its residents recognize the loss. Often the open space is unincorporated land, which gives an illusory sense of protection. As the suburb or its neighbors expand, this rural edge and open land

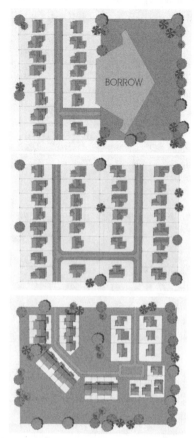

Figure 3-25. Clustering to create borrowed space.

Figure 3-26. Suburban town center with landscaped plaza. Lake Forest, Illinois.

within the community disappears. With cluster development, seen on the bottom of figure 3-25, each development preserves the needed open space and is not dependent on borrowing open space from vacant land that can be developed in the future.

It is also possible to design nonresidential areas that have a suburban character. Figure 3-26 shows a central business area in Lake Forest, Illinois, with a park forming a central square. A second approach for commercial is to use lots that are similar to those of single-family, with a well-landscaped front yard and screened parking in the rear (see figure 3-27). Even industry may be designed with a suburban character, as illustrated in figure 3-28.

For both residential and nonresidential types, open spaces are structuring elements that can be used to define neighborhoods and clusters of development. When using common open space in residential development, it is generally important to have it in the 30–40 percent range and to maximize the number of homes that have views. Using the natural drainage pattern in the area is one way for this to be achieved and to provide continuous greenways. A large, regular block of open space is less desirable because there is less perimeter available for homes to have views. Borrowed views are obviously most effective when they can be seen from the individual living units. It requires care to lay out developments in order to provide views and make use of the natural assets of the site. These views can become part of the marketing strategy of the developer and can increase the value of the lots. In fact, sound design will result in lots that have premium prices because of their relationship to open space. Even a shopping center can be developed using this approach, where a village green, park land, or golf course can provide 55–65 percent open space, resulting in a very identifiable, community-scaled town center.

Congestion is generally undesirable. The real threat of congestion to suburban character is the stripping (dividing) of highway frontages into commercial lots each having access from the highway. This affects the visual character and brings traffic volumes and turning movements that ensure the roads are busy. If the area is residential, an arterial spacing of two-lane roads every mile will generally be adequate.[18] At three dwelling units per acre, the spacing needs to be near a half mile. The introduction of auto-urban strip commercial totally destroys this, because instead of an acre generating thirty trips per day, it can be upward of a thousand per day.[19] Thus, even taking commuting into account, suburban areas are not likely to be congested. When suburbs introduce urban or auto-urban strips into the mix, however, the potential for congestion is increased by many orders of magnitude.

While it is possible to design a suburb that is entirely sub-urban in character, the historical pattern of a suburban residential community with an urban node still makes a great deal of sense from a planning perspective. In general suburban nodes will support community-scale commercial nodes as a town center. As the scale reaches the district or sector levels, however, it is not likely to retain a suburban character for the entire area.

Suburban communities provide the full range of services. Public water and sewer are essential, and the water service needs to be capable of fighting, rather than containing, a fire. This means not only adequate pressure, but also lines and storage capacity so that the water can be delivered for a sustained period. The level of police and other services is similar to urban levels. While there is at least the perception of less crime in the suburbs, it does not significantly affect the level of effort per thousand population. The citizens expect a full level of services identical to those in urban areas, and would be upset if there was a lowering of the quality or quantity of those services.

Figure 3-27. Commercial with landscaped front yards. Pebble Beach, California.

Figure 3-28. Suburban industrial. Seattle, Washington.

Estate

Estate is the low-density type of sub-urban community. It is most familiar in its historical form, where the borrowed open space is contained on each individual lot. The estate was a real escape from the city, and homes were isolated on large properties. The term "estate" was chosen because of the historical lifestyle of this character type (see figure 3-29). Some have objected to the term "estate" because of the implication that it is an area for the wealthy. Indeed, for most of history only the wealthy were able to maintain large estates on the edge of the city. Only they could afford to displace farmland with villas that allowed their families to live away from the city for at least part of the year. In major metropolitan areas, estate communities are generally higher-income areas. In terms of land economics,

Figure 3-29. Formal estate residential. Lake Forest, Illinois.

Figure 3-30. Informal estate residential. Clark County, Ohio.

while property in estate areas may be somewhat cheaper on a per-acre basis than in areas zoned suburban, it is significantly more expensive on a per-dwelling-unit basis. The larger lot means more streets, electric, cable, gas, and sometimes water lines that must be built for each unit. As a result, it is highly likely that dwelling costs will be significantly higher.[20]

All the elements that make borrowed space effective in suburban environments are also important in estate environments. The garden quality of the landscaping remains critical, but a more natural feel is desired in many communities. The fact that communities enact comprehensive plans when the areas are only partially developed leads estate residents to confuse the borrowed rural character as the community's actual character. Thus preserving natural areas (see figure 3-30) or adding elements that have a rural flavor (e.g., horse fences) is important and should be part of the estate strategy. A landscaping strategy is to abandon the street tree requirement for one that creates hedgerows, which are far more effective at screening buildings from view. Density, however, is much lower than in suburban areas, with averages of 0.5 to 0.25 dwelling units per acre (two to four acres per dwelling unit) being common. In one type of estate area, keeping horses is important to owners. These equestrian-oriented developments need lots of three-to-five acres minimum for a house, yard, and land for the horse, so these have lower densities. The actual density is quite sensitive to the area's land cover. If forest is the cover, densities can be higher than for land converted from agriculture or prairie.

The estate, like the suburb, is an escape from the city and other urban places. With their larger lots, estate areas also pretend to rural qualities. The estate character can be achieved via two different methods. The conventional, large, single-family lot approach provides an estate character with little requirement for common open space (0–10 percent).[21] The density in this model should generally be less than 0.45 dwelling units per acre (a two-acre or larger lot). The second method relies on clustering. Clustering borrowed open space is an effective manner of protecting natural resources or promoting an image that has a strong rural flavor. Open space may be in the same 30–40 percent range as in suburban, or it may exceed 50 percent, as in Randall Arendt's conservation development.[22] At these higher open space levels, the character nears the transition to rural.

There is too much development to really maintain a rural character, but to city dwellers it looks like living in the country even though there is insufficient land to maintain agriculture.

Many estate areas are totally residential, traditional bedroom communities. Because of the lower intensity, the land area needed to support even convenience- or neighborhood-level commercial activity centers is very large. Economics dictates that these uses are less likely to be built to the estate character. Commercial and business uses are expected to constitute less than 1 percent of the total land area. As with suburban, most commercial land uses can be designed to provide an estate character (see figure 3-31). High-end corporate offices and institutional uses are the most likely types of nonresidential uses that may be willing to pay a premium to locate and build in estate areas (see figure 3-32). The open space or landscaped surface for nonresidential needs to be 65–85 percent. Many estate communities rely on other communities to provide shopping or, like suburban areas, have a small urban node to provide these services. Estate areas will have far more commuters traveling out of the community to work than do suburban areas.

Since encounter levels are very low, the neighboring patterns of very young children can be affected because the lower density makes distances between friends too great for easy walking much beyond the block or cluster. This means young children must often be taken to visit by parents. For older children, the bicycle, skateboard, or in-line skates offer greater mobility. Clustering provides the potential for greater neighboring because of smaller lot sizes. Privacy is at a high level even outdoors, due to the larger lot. Historically, many estates were surrounded by trees or hedges, which made for total privacy. Clustered development somewhat reduces outdoor privacy, but this is offset by greater neighboring. With clustering, a common sewer system becomes essential. In some cases, extending public sewers is the best solution to providing sewer service to smaller lots. In other cases, the answer can be private land-treatment systems.[23]

Congestion is totally unacceptable for estate areas. The estate character will be disrupted even by major regional arterials that traverse such communities. Residents fight the widening of the roads because of fear that the increased congestion will

Figure 3-31. Estate commercial with wooded site. New Seabury, Massachusetts.

Figure 3-32. Estate office with 80 percent open space. Riverwoods, Illinois.

destroy their lifestyle. Paradoxically, refusing to widen the roads adds to congestion. Estate areas need design standards that protect residents from regional traffic.

The major distinguishing elements between suburban and estate are the density and service levels provided to residents. Water and sewer services are generally private in estate areas, rather than public as in suburban. The well and sewerage disposal provided on the individual lot typically requires lot sizes in excess of one acre. There are, however, some notable exceptions to private wells; there are large areas of the nation where rural water utilities exist. For water the key is not public or private, but the level of service. Rural water districts by and large do not provide water with sufficient pressure and flow to fight fires. Thus insurance rates are much higher in these areas because the homes will generally be total losses in the event of a fire. Both individual wells and rural water districts provide a lower level or service than in suburban and urban areas. Crime tends to be lower and police services are often lower as well. Narrower roads built to rural standards are typical. In some estate communities the roads are privatized, reducing further the tax demands of the local government.[24] The reduced level of services may turn out to be an important planning strategy associated with the estate type of development.

While it is possible to design most uses to estate character, the reality is that most estate areas will be residential; if there is a commercial component, a small urban node makes sense but would clearly be limited to convenience–or possibly community–level services.

RURAL CLASS

The third community character class is rural. As was true between the urban and sub-urban classes, the rural class represents a very large shift in character. In rural environments, space dominates to the point that it appears to be infinite, extending to the horizon or beyond. The built environment is minimized and relegated to the background. Infinite space is borrowed space taken to an extreme. The quality of the space changes as well, becoming a true landscape. The term "landscape" has been chosen because in rural environments, as in a landscape painting or photography, a pastoral or natural scene extends to the horizon. The interest is in the land and sky; buildings, if visible at all, are in the distant background. The horizon line should be unbroken by buildings. A pure landscape has no sign of human settlements or development, as in figure 3-33, where natural elements—mountains, trees, and river—constitute the ground-based interest all the way to the horizon. In figure 3-34 the village is in the background, at the base of a hill, so the horizon is unbroken by buildings. In the United States, the pattern of farms means that there will be farm buildings in any pastoral landscape. In figure 3-35 there are farm buildings in the middle ground that are highly visible and break the plane of the horizon. In most of the United States, however, farmhouses, barns, and silos are seen as an integral part of the agricultural landscape, so they are not as intrusive as a subdivision would be.

The horizon, not the skyline created by man-made structures, is an essential element of a landscape. Any residential building in the foreground or middle ground that breaks the plain of the horizon line, as in figure 3-36, is a problem because the eye is drawn to the building rather than the landscape as a whole. While it certainly is appealing to have a house with a view over the landscape, the problem is that too often the rest of the population must look at the buildings built on the ridgeline or hilltop. There is a major exception to this discussion in Europe, where the farmers generally lived in hamlets or villages. European hill towns, as seen in figure 3-37, were built on hilltops and not only break the horizon, but also violate the rule to keep buildings off high ground. There are two reasons this works in Europe. First, just as Americans ignore farm structures breaking the horizon, Europeans see these as belonging to the landscape because they have been there for hundreds of years. Second, planning in Europe has retained open space and sharp edges, so the rural quality of the overall landscape is not disrupted. Even when the village was sited on a ridge for defense, it seems natural because of the vast supply of rural land and compact settlement pattern. Like the farm buildings in this country, these rural communities seem to belong. A major element in rural design is controlling high points, as discussed in the rural chapter of the second book, *A Guide to Planning for Community Character*.

Figure 3-33. Rural landscape. Near Anchorage, Alaska.

Figure 3-34. Village in background. Outside Arvada, Colorado.

Figure 3-35. Large farm buildings viewed as part of landscape. Door County, Wisconsin.

Figure 3-36. Home on low ridge disturbs skyline. Nantucket, Massachusetts.

Figure 3-37. Fortified town on hill. Trujillo, Spain.

As discussed in chapter 2, there are freestanding rural communities, hamlets, and villages that would be classified as urban or suburban when character is measured within the boundaries of the settlement. Freestanding communities are rural communities. They are widely spaced in the rural region due to economic need. In a rural region with hamlets and villages, the open space ratio would approach 100 percent.

The pastoral rural area may be viewed as a human ecological unit. Each farm is an industry, a basic unit for the production of food and fiber. Modern mechanized agriculture often involves farming a thousand or more acres, and ranches are measured in square miles. The rural hamlet or village functions as a service node for a rural area. As a result, the small, agricultural, freestanding communities have a stronger economy than the population of the settlement would indicate, since it services a surrounding agricultural population.

Land use is an important element in defining rural character types. While use mixes are important indicators in the suburban or urban classes, all three rural types are distinguished by use. The agricultural type is defined by producers of food and fiber. The natural type is a biological reserve, while the countryside district is intended as an exurban residential area that permits agriculture or natural areas to continue.

As with all other forms of settlements, rural areas have been affected by technology in the form of the automobile. Mechanization of farm equipment has vastly increased the land that a single farmer can farm, to the point where many grain farmers till a thousand or more acres (in contrast to the forty-acre farmstead of the late nineteenth century). Old farmsteads left over from the era of smaller farms have either been abandoned, given to children who do not farm, or sold to exurbanites. The automobile has made possible the new lifestyle of exurban living. These people truly desire to live in the country (even though this character is borrowed), not a suburb. Some want land for horses or other rural activities. While they move to rural areas for a rural lifestyle, it has generally been a short-lived environment, because as others follow the character changes to a sub-urban type.

A family is generally isolated on their own farm, so the nearest neighbors will be a minimum of a quarter mile away—

beyond easy walking distance.[25] Newcomers seek similar isolation, even if all they own is a one-acre lot. The result is an altered pattern of neighboring. The population must gather to socialize, be it at a church, store, post office, or rural tavern. Neighboring as a near-daily interaction does not occur. Encounter ratios are very low and the frequency of social interaction rare. The term "congestion" is meaningless in rural areas because the densities are too low to generate it. Only in natural areas is environmental preservation really possible, since agriculture has totally altered the landscape. Rural areas generally demand less services from government; accordingly, police, fire, and other services are provided at a lower level.

Countryside

Countryside must accommodate two distinct populations: exurban residents and those who work the land. By this very fact, the exurbanite displaces a portion of the rural landscape and the area available for agriculture. The exurbanite usually works elsewhere, although some come to countryside areas for a second home or for recreational purposes. Some residents work or tend the land in some fashion. Even more so than sub-urban populations, the exurban population is made up of commuters, with only a few self-employed individuals working from their homes. The farmer, rancher, forestry worker, or others whose jobs involve either agriculture or managing natural areas are residents because it is their place of employment. In the United States, those involved in agriculture live on the land they farm. Forestry or environmental employees have the ability to live in communities or isolated lots.

Historically, countryside has been an ephemeral type. Exurbanites seeking to live in rural areas often strip off road frontage, as seen in figure 3-38a. Its residents enjoy living in the country, but their one-to-five-acre lots do not provide for rural character. Figure 3-38b overlays the lot pattern of one-plus-acre lots, an estate lot size that represents the seeds of destruction of the countryside character. The rural character of a community is entirely borrowed from surrounding land owned by others. All the lots were stripped off the frontage and each blocks a

Figure 3-38a. Countryside development. Door County, Wisconsin.

Figure 3-38b. Lotting pattern shown will not protect character.

view of the landscape. If countryside is to be something other than an ephemeral rural type, the exurban development pattern must be altered.

Without dramatic intervention, an area of countryside will evolve, eventually becoming a form of sub-urban or urban. Depending on growth pressure, that evolution may take anywhere from twenty to sixty years. Aside from metropolitan areas and tourist destinations where there is little population growth, areas may remain in a countryside state almost indefinitely as long as population growth is very slow. The process starts with stripping a few lots off the road, which initially appears to do little damage. Once this area is discovered, stripping increases and is followed by small subdivisions. It is then only a matter of time before the character changes. Any municipality that seeks to maintain a countryside environment in the face of development pressure will need to design a strategy that limits development to a small portion of the total area.

As with most threats to character, this is not recognized until it is too late. As farms have grown larger, the excess farmstead housing was seen as a place for the farmer's children or parents to live. The occasional exurbanite who bought these homes was also not seen as a threat. Likewise the subdivision of a lot, whether for a child, parent, or for sale, was not seen as a threat because it was helping to keep a family together or make a little extra money. The exurbanite seeking rural living, however, is the leading edge of urbanization. Over time subdivisions are promoted as rural living and the area is doomed.

Countryside, as discussed here, is a permanent character type. It is a rural environment whose express purpose is to permit enough development to be attractive as an exurban living area, while limiting the amount of land developed in order to preserve rural character and agriculture. Countryside not only provides a unique residential living environment, but can also serve as a major structuring element in the design of metropolitan or independent regions. The "star" or "finger" metropolitan plans of forty years ago give clear evidence that these planners understood the value of permanent rural areas as part of the metropolitan framework (see the discussion of metropolitan forms in chapter 4). Rural types were understood as valuable to relieve the sameness of the suburbs by providing green corridors that give shape to the metropolitan area.

The conscious use of the paradox of clustering is an essential element in creating the countryside character. If each subdivision preserves an appropriate amount of rural land within its boundaries in addition to the residential area, a countryside character is preserved. Extreme clustering, with more than 80 percent of the land in open space, has the potential to retain active farms or large-scale natural areas in the face of exurban pressures. Figure 3-39 shows the view from a road into a fully developed countryside, the Fields of Long Grove, designed by Kendig Keast Collaborative. There is about four hundred feet of prairie between the road and the hedgerow, behind which the development's homes are clustered. This strategy preserves sufficient rural land, in the form of prairie and hedgerow (natural), to ensure a countryside character. If the area is forested, the preservation of countryside character is easier because clusters of development may be more easily hidden. Figure 3-40 illustrates a home on a very large lot with the home hidden by trees. The freestanding rural hamlet or village is a naturally occurring example of extreme clustering. These communities were surrounded by a working landscape of farms. In order to replicate this pattern, cluster regulations will be required

The extreme cluster provides some neighboring potential. The densities are lower than with estate, so congestion and encounter levels are very low. It is best that these clusters have their own well and sewer system serving the entire cluster rather than private wells and sewage on each lot. These would typically be owned by the development rather than government.

Figure 3-39. Fully developed site. Fields of Long Grove, Long Grove, Illinois.

Figure 3-40. Countryside character: very large lot with home in woodland. Bucks County, Pennsylvania.

In an ideal world, the only residents in agriculture or natural areas would be those employed there: farmers, ranchers, and people engaged in forestry, hunting, trapping, or protection of the natural environment. In Europe, planning and zoning have the ability to achieve this ideal. In the United States, political considerations make it difficult or impossible to do the same. In most areas it is not a legal issue because agriculture is a legitimate use of rural land.[26] While land for agriculture could in many states be zoned for between forty and one thousand acres per dwelling unit or exclusive agricultural use, this remains politically difficult anywhere there is significant development pressure. This would be more risky for natural areas as there is less value associated with the use. Clustering will be used for these districts even though it is clearly a compromise solution.

Agricultural

The agricultural environment is one that produces food and fiber. It is the basic function and rationale of the agricultural area to be a primary production unit. Unlike other land uses, agriculture combines the industry and home in a single unit. The agricultural community is made up of the production units and essential support uses. The production of food and fiber is a basic industry, producing odor, noise, dust, and using chemicals, making it best that residential is not mixed with agricultural uses. The primary inhabitants in agricultural areas are likely to be livestock (see figure 3-41). This stands in sharp contrast to the countryside, where both exurban residential and agriculture are equal goals.

In design, agricultural areas are quite similar to countryside. Extreme clusters with more than 90 percent open space and hamlets or villages with 95 percent open space are the ideals that should be sought. The area should appear as a landscape, albeit one that is designed by humans to produce their food or fiber. Whether the agricultural use is pasture or crops, the landscape should resemble the one shown in figure 3-42. To accomplish this, any nonagricultural buildings need to be located well in the background or be very heavily screened.

Figure 3-41. Agriculture grazing land. Teton County, Wyoming.

Figure 3-42. Agricultural cropland. Lake County, Illinois.

Natural

The natural area is the third type in the rural class. The land use in these areas is predominantly natural habitat. It may be forest (see figure 3-43), savannah, old field, prairie, wetland, a mix of forest and meadows (see figure 3-44), or another natural system. The primary inhabitants of the natural area are wildlife. If development is a political necessity, extreme clustering and very low density are essential. Visually, natural areas are seen as landscape. The type of natural ecosystem or biome will present vastly different visual characteristics and present very different design and site-planning issues. The forest is the least demanding, as the lakeshore development in figure 3-45 illustrates. Where forests are the primary land cover, one rarely sees the horizon, except from an occasional hill- or ridgetop (since trees block the view). For example, redwood forests are described as being cathedral-like, with large, towering trees that limit views. Where the land cover is savannah, prairie, or desert, preserving the landscape and horizon becomes far more difficult. The strategy for open natural landscapes is similar to agriculture: extreme cluster development and placement in the background or in heavily screened areas.

The use and function of the natural area are the major elements that distinguish it from other rural community types. The natural area is intended to be left as untouched by human habitation and use as is legally possible, as it provides natural habitats for plant and animal species. In the natural area, the rationale for human intrusion applies to publicly owned parks or natural areas. Tourism or vacation housing interests are nearly always attracted to these areas of natural beauty. Placing such areas under pressure to provide housing.

SPECIAL CHARACTER TYPES

The eight character types are generally adequate to cover the planning of much of a municipality. There are a number of land uses, however, that do not fit well in the community character topology. Some of these are not to be considered communities that provide places to live. Heavier industry and mining are clearly in this group. Refineries, tank farms, concrete plants,

Figure 3-43. Natural forest character. Door County, Wisconsin.

Figure 3-44. Wildlife inhabitants of natural area. Humboldt County, California.

Figure 3-45. Residential development retaining natural character. Pine Crest, California.

Figure 3-46. Maritime heavy industry. Sturgeon Bay, Wisconsin.

Figure 3-47. Small-scale heavy industry. Annapolis, Maryland.

Figure 3-48. College campus. Sherman, Texas.

power plants, or shipyards (see figure 3-46) are examples of uses that look more like machines than buildings. Other industrial areas are characterized by excessive outdoor storage (see figure 3-47). Others uses, while they might conceivably be broken into the eight types, are poor fits, and often are very special uses (e.g., airports and military bases). These last two have specific nuisances associated with them that make them unique and often beyond local zoning control.

There are a few uses that bridge character types but are so particular that they should be classed independently. Universities and colleges fall into this category, as they have characteristics of urban, auto-urban, and suburban mixed together. The buildings are often large and very urban in character, but the campus design often includes open areas so that open space is often suburban-like (see figure 3-48). Other parts of campus have extensive parking, an auto-urban characteristic. Because of the special nature of this land use type, these institutions are clearly best left as a separate character type. Mining and maritime concerns are other uses that may need to be treated as special character types in some communities.

CHAPTER 4 | *Community and Regional Forms*

Communities can be designed in three different forms: compositional, group, and mega. Somewhat like buildings, communities can be classified by their structural framework. Buildings built with post and beam, balloon frame, masonry, vault, or dome are structurally very different from one another. Human settlements also have a structural framework formed by buildings, streets, and spaces. The manner in which these components are assembled can be called community forms.

Metropolitan regions, or areas around cities, are often composed of many municipalities. Regional planning at one time was concerned with the form or plan of a region as a whole. Planners tried to give the metropolitan region a physical form with developed areas, and they set aside rural areas to be a permanent part of the region as it grows. Over the last forty years, however, regions have largely grown as ever-expanding areas, with all rural areas lost in successive planning efforts. The result is that most regions are boringly the same. It is time to revisit metropolitan forms, which will be done in the second part of this chapter.

COMMUNITY FORMS

A great many communities were conceived and built as a single form. This is particularly true of hamlets and villages. Historically, larger towns and cities have one form overlaid on another.[1] This can result in the creation of a better community if the forms are mixed to create a more complex order and sense of structure. Both Paris and Venice have benefited from such refinements. Baron Haussmann's redesign of Paris (1852–70) is a notable example of this because it created the radial boulevards and uniform streetscape that unite the city. But a redesign is not always an improvement. For example, Savannah began with a great plan that was abandoned as the city grew beyond the bounds of that original vision; today, neighborhoods are no longer blessed or identified with squares, and commercial development sprawls along major roads.

The three basic types of structural forms—compositional, group, and mega[2]—(see figure 4-1) may be applied to any size community or part of a community, but are most useful when applied to the design of smaller-scale communities (no larger than the freestanding town). The forms, which are distinctly different in appearance, can be considered design concepts for assembling or organizing a community.

The group form, such as a European village, is where there is no overall plan, but each new building extends the street or expands space to foster the movement of people or goods. Compositional forms (most American cities) have a preplanned pattern of streets and blocks that are divided into building lots. Mega forms are communities in a single structure, such as a pueblo. While most planning today is compositional in nature, the other forms provide additional ways to organize a community and provide a memorable identity. For each, the manner in which a plan is conceived or developed differs. Examples of group and compositional forms can be found in nearly every country. The mega form is relatively rare, and while theoretically unlimited in scale, the examples are all fairly small in size, and many are old. So while there are three structural forms in practice, nearly all modern design and planning is with the compositional form. We are more familiar with group forms from visiting Europe.

A community with *compositional form* is planned along a predetermined pattern of streets. This may be done by design, as with Baron Haussmann's redesign of Paris, or as a result of surveyors plotting townships, sections, quarter sections, and further dividing into lots for quick, easy sales. Greek and Roman colonies represent an early application of the grid to a new city. There are a number of street patterns that can be applied to compositional forms, as will be discussed below.

While compositional form is the result of deliberate design or real estate decisions, *group form* is organic, derived from an assortment of individual decisions over time. Historically, the

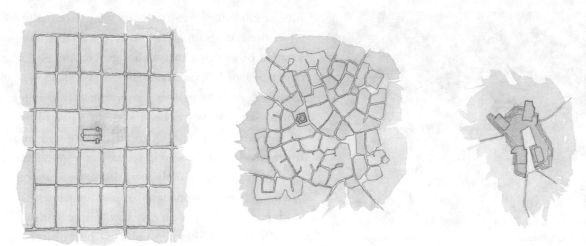

Figure 4-1. Community forms: compositional, group, mega.

builder of each building would take into account previous buildings, topography, and the desired functions and activities of the building, and use standard construction techniques and materials to build a structure. The group form is typified by vernacular architecture and is found in small rural communities, hamlets, villages, and towns. Medieval towns will be the most familiar example to many people, such as Assisi, Italy, or Rothonburg, O.T., Germany (figure 2-5). Unlike compositional form, there is no designer creating an overall plan. As buildings are added, they extend existing spaces or streets.

The *mega form* evolved from a defensive community that exists in a single building, like a pueblo or castle. More recently, architects revisited this form after World War II in books and concept plans. It is a development form to be applied at a small scale, such as the hamlet/block or village/neighborhood. It is advocated as another way to achieve very high intensities on little land through a mixed-use structure, combining what normally would be many separate buildings into one unit.

Compositional Form

Compositional form is the one most familiar to citizens, urban designers, and planners. The planned pattern is usually a geometric form, which designers, engineers, surveyors, or architects use to structure a community by laying out the right-of-way or centerline of roads. The roads create blocks, which are

Figure 4-2. Blocks are divided into lots. Palm Beach County, Florida.

further subdivided into lots for buildings (see figure 4-2). Ideally, a functional diagram is created before drafting the plan for the location of key elements within the community.[3] The plan for new Greek or Roman towns laid out the location of important functions such as market, government, and religion. In the United States, surveyors laid the western part of the nation out into sections of a mile square. These were aggregated up to townships and subdivided into quarters.[4] The surveyors did not lay out roads; they simply provided maps that could be replicated, and the section or quarter-section lines often became roads because that was an easy way to access properties.

Buddhist or Shinto temples in China or Japan and college campuses in the United States are powerful compositional forms, but the design is not street-based; rather buildings, spaces, and paths to direct or channel movement are contained within a complex and do not relate to nearby spaces. Urban renewal has been a frequent user of compositional form, creating a precinct or area within a larger community structure. Modern office complexes and college campuses are often structured in the compositional form and may be quite separate from the community. At the smallest scale, compositional form may be applied to a group of buildings if each one is carefully sited in formal relationship to others in the group.

A great strength of the compositional form is the power of the designer to structure the community, whether it is the streets of Paris or St. Marks Square in Venice. Today's rapid pace of development and the "abandon and move on" mentality have weakened compositional form. Another barrier to creating compositional forms is conflict of egos, with each architect or user competing to make their own building the architectural centerpiece, or worse turning buildings into corporate logos or signs. Designers in previous centuries never had to worry about a fast-food restaurant competing for attention with the cathedral or town hall. The organizational structure of a community must in some fashion dictate which buildings will be in the background and which will be prominent.

Ideally, a whole community would be laid out using the compositional form; in reality, it is generally limited to new, planned communities. Even then, as the planned community grows beyond its original bounds the pattern is often discontinued. Many of the early rail suburbs had a single developer who did the master plan, but this was not followed as other developers expanded the community. Nearly all municipal plans ignore the neighborhood-level street pattern. By default, the neighborhood plan is nearly always left to the developers, each laying out a subdivision, the sum of which becomes a neighborhood. This means that whole neighborhoods are not designed, even though they are the basic building block of communities, which is a root cause of the lack of connectivity in community design. It is exceedingly rare to find a comprehensive plan—such as the one implemented in the city of Franklin, Wisconsin (see figure 4-3)—where every neighborhood is planned in detail, down to the location of streets and lots.[5] For the most part, planners today allow individual developers to plan their own projects, hoping that a real neighborhood will result. Neighborhood planning needs to be done by the municipality once again.

A more difficult task than planning a new community is that of the planner working in the context of an existing municipality. The community already exists, and a small town or village is growing. The planner is charged with developing a comprehensive plan for the community's growth. The goal is to make a compositional form, starting with an existing pattern of rural roads, into which the new growth will be directed. While the Franklin example may be too extreme, the presence of a drainage pattern and other physical features suggest some major design elements that can structure part of the neighborhood plan. The property or parcel map that shows the existing division of land within a neighborhood into lots can also provide some guidance. For a neighborhood to be a success it must have a pattern of streets that provide internal circulation, which means somebody creates an overall plan. An important element is at least a sketch plan, if not a precise plan, for the street pattern within a superblock bounded by arterials, which creates a good neighborhood design. The key elements are storm drainage, sewer service, proposed land uses, an internal circulation system, and how the homes relate to the existing exterior or bounding streets.

Parks and open spaces are important in a compositional plan, but they rarely seem to be the structuring elements. This should not degrade their importance. Even in the most urban community character type, at least some open spaces are important, and they become more so in suburban character types, where borrowed space is critical to the garden-like character. In

Figure 4-3. Neighborhood plan. Franklin, Wisconsin.

Figure 4-4. Squares used as organization. Savannah, Georgia.

Figure 4-5. Parkway and drainage used to organize. Florence, South Carolina.

Figure 4-6. Very long, heavily landscaped cul-de-sac island. Fields of Long Grove, Long Grove, Illinois.

suburban areas, parks or common open space can easily be designed into a development, while government may have to buy park sites in urban areas. It is far better if they are part of the original design of the community form. Savannah's parks (see figure 4-4) are an excellent example of open space providing structure: the regular placement of open space, which interrupts the grid streets, creates squares; the squares have names and provide a strong identity to neighborhoods of the city.

Park land or green space can be used in other ways. For example, it may be more natural and provide for views, trails, and drainage, as seen in figure 4-5. Linear open spaces or parks can also provide large-scale structure that is richer than a street pattern alone. In sub-urban environments especially, open space can become a structuring element as important as the roads, because it can be 25–40 percent of the total land area. A parkway (a street with a landscaped center island) breaks up traffic and provides green space in the fronts of homes. A variation on this is where a cul-de-sac is used to create green space, as in figure 4-6. Figure 4-7 shows a large, parklike cul-de-sac island on the right, an enlarged island on the left, and near the center an island that extends nearly the length of the cul-de-sac. This can be important in defining boundaries, as well as providing identity. In figures 4-7 and 4-8, the structuring element of this subdivision plan was open space used to separate clusters. The objective is to provide each house with a view of open space. In urban areas, ravines or topographic conditions can create open spaces that serve a similar role. In particular, these corridors can provide city or regional greenways.

There are three major patterns of compositional form in use: grid, radial, and curvilinear. There has been discussion of hexagonal street layouts, but no serious attempt to use them. Ebenezer Howard's garden city model suggested radial streets with circumferential cross streets.[6] Curvilinear streets are curved rather than straight (see figure 4-9), and often have cul-de-sacs around them to more efficiently use the land. The curved street creates a design challenge because connecting to a grid pattern can be difficult. The grid street pattern can be extended nearly infinitely, and is limited primarily by water bodies or topography that prohibit the extension of the street.

Radial streets are generally straight and are organized around an important element at the center, such as a park, building, or monument. Annapolis, Maryland, seen in figure 4-10, has buildings occupying the circles, which act as the centroids of the radial pattern; the building or object is generally visible down each radial street. The schematic plan of a garden city and the resulting pattern of streets is shown in figure 4-11. The concept was a simple series of concentric rings, with the center containing commercial, civic, and other important city elements; residential density would decline in the outer rings, and the entire city would be surrounded by a greenbelt.

While there are models of neighborhoods that address the placement of land uses and how they function, such as those of Clarence Perry or Clarence Stein,[7] there has been too little thought about how the neighborhood is changing. Christopher Alexander's *A Pattern Language* attempts to provide a wide range of rules, representing a useful starting point for the development of a series of compositional forms from towns to homes. Scale and character type can assist in developing a rational, municipal-level plan, where the thoroughfare plan (showing arterial and collector roads) generally defines the neighborhoods in the municipality and identifies the nonresidential areas, providing a good basis for a municipal plan using the compositional form.

Group Forms

The first human settlements were group forms.[8] These early habitations were based on a specific building type, whether they were originally movable forms like tepees and yurts, or more permanent structures of wood or masonry. Their variety is great, from an African village with large, central spaces in which to shelter their animals from the local wildlife, to the medieval village. Group forms were created by individual living groups or families using the vernacular architecture (styles, materials, and construction methods that befit the community). An example is seen in figure 4-12, with the characteristic barrel roof buildings of the Greek Islands. Figure 4-13 shows half-timbered construction with steep roofs, characteristic of German towns.

Structure of Group Forms

In compositional form, the streets and spaces create the blocks that are divided into building sites. In the group form, the

Figure 4-7. Cluster plan. Fields of Long Grove, Long Grove, Illinois.

Figure 4-8. Open space in cluster. Lake Villa, Illinois.

Figure 4-9. Curvilinear road provides natural feel. Kildeer, Illinois.

Figure 4-10. Axial streets. Annapolis, Maryland.

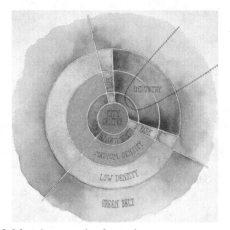

Figure 4-11. Schematic plan for garden city.

Figure 4-12. Group form on vaulted stone buildings. Santorini, Greece.

buildings structure the environment and leave space for public activities and circulation. The earliest communities made no distinction between public and private outdoor spaces. Community forms developed one building at a time. There were no planning agencies, master plans, or zoning/subdivision rules. The growth was slow, with new homes built for new generations as needed. Family and community relationships strongly influenced the building location, ensuring it was not built where it could create a circulation problem. At any point in time there were established pathways into the community, and new buildings respected those parameters. Likewise, existing activities in the spaces were respected.

The group form may be seen as organic, in that as it grows it is shaped by the environment and the gradual addition of buildings. The community grows and evolves, building by building, respecting the topography and existing pathways rather than being built to a predetermined form (figures 4-14 and 4-15). There was no thought of recontouring the site to fit a plan. As uses were needed, either a new building was built or a small area redone. Occasionally, important buildings like a church or city hall would carve out a new space, but this was a community decision, as the entire community was needed to build and support the building and space. The stone architecture provides a uniform character for the buildings.

Group forms can be found on very steep sites, so it is not uncommon that pedestrian streets consist of stairs to function on very demanding topography (see figure 4-15). In all these group forms, the community space is flexible. Streets or spaces are larger where there are other needs, such as churches, town halls, or markets. A cluster of shops may create a wider street to provide activity space that benefits their businesses. A restaurant with outdoor seating may be set back further from the street to provide space (see figure 4-16). Waterfront communities may have a shore that is simultaneously an entry point and marine industrial area for fishing boats or other maritime traffic. This results in a varied activity area open to the sea on one side. A hierarchy of streets and spaces is created by changes in the scale of building separations or by activities that require more space.

Group forms have great unity of character, because the buildings are a clear reflection of limits of building technology, available resources, topography, and social function shaping the community (rather than a reflection of the architect).[9] The buildings often share a common form or floor plan. Organic is probably a good description[10] for group form, because the buildings that are key elements appear similar to cells in microscopic photos showing plant or animal cells. Organic also fits the fact that the use of buildings often modified the existing street pattern.

The medieval city and the small communities in Europe, Asia, and North Africa provide the best examples of this type of form. As mentioned above, the Greek Islands have stone-barrel-vault architecture. In Italy and Spain the stone buildings have a common appearance. In Britain and Germany buildings are often half-timbered. The exhibit and subsequent book on the theme *Architecture Without Architects*[11] focused on vernacular architectural forms and has provided exposure to the rich diversity that is possible using group forms. Modern group forms are found in the barrios of developing nations, where individual squatters carve out a building space with no planning assistance from the landowners or local governments.

A unique building tradition in Italy based on local-stone houses with vault roofs creates a form of considerable visual impact. The dry (unmortared) stonework created a sharply different form—the Trulli—with a conical stone roof shape, demonstrating the power of local communities to create identity.[12] It is the repetition of a basic form, each with subtle variations, that gives the community its visual unity yet enough variety to avoid monotony.

While the example chosen is a stone building form, the group form comes in all manner of materials and styles. Buildings of wood, clay, thatch, and stone can be found from the early civilizations[13] of Mesopotamia and Egypt up to modern times.

Design with the Group Form

Is it possible to design a modern group form? There is certainly considerable difficulty in seeking to apply the principles of the group form to a planned community of any significant size, because a developer-built group form of a larger scale requires preplanning and the invention of a new form of zoning and subdivision. The architecture and sale of a group form presents additional design challenges. Creating a realistic community where

Figure 4-13. Half-timbered homes. Tübingen, Germany.

Figure 4-14. Pedestrian street. Beget, Spain.

Figure 4-15. Street of stairs to account for topography. Hydra, Greece.

Figure 4-16. Widened street for restaurant. Hydra, Greece.

the building architecture fosters a strong sense of harmony is important. Too often, production-builder attempts at replicating a past style look phony, and that could lead to rejection in the marketplace. To provide interest and richness of community character, many small details or plan variations will need to be developed. The architect and mass builder will be seriously challenged to replicate this feeling. The smallest freestanding community is most amenable to the attempt as it is the easiest to manage.

Preplanning a group form is the first challenge. There are two approaches that need to be combined. The first addresses the street system, which in order to receive approval by a local government will have to receive variances from subdivision standards, and that requires detailed planning and engineering. This is the antithesis of an organic process.

Subdivision standards and the Transect require rigid street cross sections. The group form would have to permit some combination of varied street width. This can be done by building in traffic-calming width changes and varying the type of on-street parking from none, on one side, on two sides, and using both parallel and angled parking. The width and placement of sidewalks and the presence or absence of parkway planting are additional tools that can be used to create a unique and varying organic street.

The second element addresses the setback. Zoning regulations set up a situation where the buildings are all lined up on the setback line. The SmartCode[14] even requires buildings be built to the setback or sidewalk line. For single-family, detached group forms, the setbacks should be abandoned in favor of building pads. The building pad is a house location on a lot to create interest, which is selected on each lot rather than being set by minimum, front, side, and rear yard requirements. Thus one lot can require that the building be located near the front property line, while others may be set back as much as twenty feet in an urban situation. This permits house-to-house variations (even for townhouses) to achieve the feel of a vernacular street. Going along with this may be a set of guidelines that provides for different types of intrusions into the front setback to again encourage diversity. The combination of both street flexibility and building pads should enable a vernacular streetscape to be created in urban areas.

In estate situations the building pad can achieve a nearly random appearance because the larger lots provide for greatly differing pads from lot to lot. In this sort of setting, sidewalks are rare and the street presents less of a challenge than in urban areas. Suburban areas will be somewhat easier to work with than urban ones.

From the pure design point of view, working with the land rather than reengineering it is critical. One principle is that the streets work with the existing topography and do not require the site to be mass graded.[15] It has now become standard practice to mass grade sites, which destroys the ability to develop an organic design. In general, cow-path design (where roads follow the high ground and wind across topography) is desirable. Working with topography and limiting grading of lots will require home foundations to be stepped, which creates a more organic feel of buildings growing out of the land. The organic approach is also better environmentally. Normal engineering practice has increasingly been based on total regrading of the entire site to facilitate subsurface storm-water systems, which means destruction of existing tree cover, increased erosion, and more rapid runoff.

Curvilinear cul-de-sac or small loop streets are desirable, as the low-traffic volumes permit narrower streets. One lane will serve a maximum of seven or eight units. Very narrow sections or sharp curves can serve as traffic-calming features. Creating an island in a street to preserve a large tree, rather than cutting it down to create a straight street, creates a traffic-calming island and introduces an organic feeling to the street.

The way parking is handled can also introduce randomness. Some sections might prohibit parking, another might have parallel parking, and yet a third could use angled or perpendicular bays, which results in a varying of right-of-way. Another technique is the mews, where homes front on an open space rather than a street and cars reach the home via an alley.

Yet another tool is the placement of the sidewalk, sometimes on the curb and in other cases behind a parkway strip. Lastly, preplanned spaces and a minimum and average right-of-way width are required. The curve radii that govern street alignment could be made irregular or stepped as another technique to provide the organic character. Figure 4-17 uses attached atrium houses, alleys, varied street parking, and mews to create a block in group form.

The second approach is to begin with a basic lot and house form. There needs to be variation in the width and shape of lots.

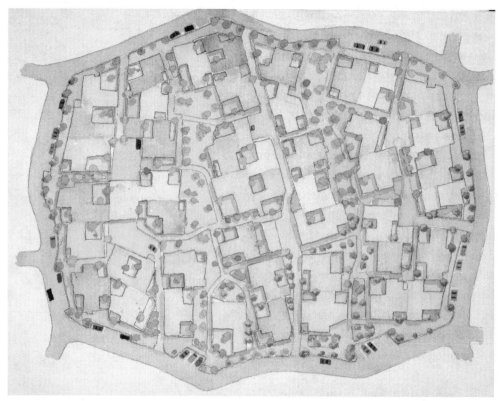

Figure 4-17. Concept plan for new group form.

Figure 4-18. Entrance to group form subdivision. Columbus, Ohio.

One way to do this with width is to return to selling lots in modules of ten, fifteen, twenty, or more feet. This was done by early speculators and surveyors, which enabled more people to buy the land in smaller, more affordable lots. It results in communities where lot size is quite variable, creating diversity in house size. Another approach is to require a mix of three or more widths per block. These techniques are best adapted to smaller lots and attached housing. Small single-family lots, patio, atrium, and townhouse variants are ideal for the creation of interest in a group form development. The use of an organic road design of varying right-of-way and pavement width, alleys, pedestrian alleys and mews, and a mix of lot sizes and orientation permits a single-family atrium house development to be a group form, as seen in figure 4-17.

Figures 4-18 through 4-20 show a development in Columbus, Ohio, that was designed to mimic a French village. While it is located in the heart of a city, it could be envisioned as a hamlet or cluster in a rural environment. The building going over the development entrance is an extreme design element, but it works to set the character of the community (figure 4-18). The development mixes setbacks and material, and uses an overall style to create a unique character. The street width is constant, though the mixed setbacks create variety.

Group form is best adapted to the small scale: hamlets, villages, and freestanding communities. It also works well for subdivisions using conservation clusters in suburban or estate areas. In both instances, the greenbelt that can be provided with a conservation cluster or freestanding community eliminates the problem of a group form attempting to mesh with an interconnected compositional development. The group form might be applied to a whole neighborhood in a composite community, but this is a larger, more complex design.

Is it possible to design a group form today? Yes, but it will not be easy. First, a developer must see this as desirable, and be willing to work to gain approval from skeptical planners, engineers, and elected officials. The most obvious candidates are small, cluster developments that can be surrounded by open space, so neighbors cannot make a meaningful complaint. Figures 4-21 through 4-25 show several parts of a small hamlet, Serenbe, in Chattahoochee Hill Country, Georgia. The character types are urban and suburban, and there is a mix of residential and commercial. Ideally, the municipality will work up the standards to address all the concerns of designers and engineers ahead of time, so the developer can concentrate on design and not have to worry about multiple redesigns to satisfy skeptics.

Mega Forms

Mega forms are human settlements where all uses are contained within a single structure. Architects and the literature often refer to these types of buildings as "mega structures." Mega structure is an accurately descriptive term but should not be limited to a community or municipality conceived and built as a single unit. It clearly can be used for smaller-scale areas; it need not be carried to the extremes envisioned by Paolo Soleri. As envisioned for future development, it is a mixed-use structure or combination of connected structures, with an internal pedestrian precinct, appropriate from a small to community scale. In all cases, this saves land, either to reduce sprawl or preserve

Figure 4-19. Varied setbacks. Columbus, Ohio.

Figure 4-20. Walled yard at corner. Columbus, Ohio.

Figure 4-21. Mixed uses on street face. Serenbe–Chattahoochee Hill County, Georgia.

Figure 4-22. Commercial center fits topography. Serenbe, Georgia.

Figure 4-23. Townhouses to sidewalk. Serenbe, Georgia.

Figure 4-24. Single-family urban. Serenbe, Georgia.

open spaces and natural areas. For many, transit will be an important element, and for larger-scale developments in the urban core it is essential. The mega form is ideal for transit-oriented developments. Environmentally, this form is important as it represents the smallest possible footprint, since the entire structure is walkable and structured around transit. The mega form is well adapted to serving a transit stop and even permitting intense economic development by expanding over time, thus providing a growing value as a destination.

Existing Mega Forms

Mega forms exhibit a dramatic change in scale when compared to group and compositional forms, which are composed of largely individual units. Historically, the mega form is most frequently seen in castles or other fortifications (see figure 4-26). The pueblos and cliff dwellings in the American Southwest are also mega forms (see figures 4-27 and 4-28). Because of their singular structure, whose exterior is most often a fortified wall, early mega structures were developed to fulfill the defensive needs of the community.

There are few modern buildings that are mega forms. Paolo Soleri, an extreme advocate of the form,[16] is building a community in the Arizona desert called Acrosanti using this technique. It has been under construction for several decades and remains only a fragment of the ultimate plan, presumably because of lack of financing. The drawing in figure 4-29 illustrates the concept. The visitor will find a collection of individual buildings that could be mistaken for a compositional form. Soleri advocated much more aggressive large-scale communities; Acrosanti was envisioned for a population of 1,500, but other plans ranged up to millions of people in a single mega structure. Kenzo Tange's plan for Tokyo envisions numerous mega structures linked over Tokyo Bay. A major problem with the mega form is that it is difficult to conceive of and finance such a structure that can easily grow and respond to market demands over time. This problem becomes increasingly severe as the scale of the development increases.

There are numerous very large buildings—including regional shopping malls, office buildings, and high-rise buildings—that are big enough to be mega structures. Some of these have proved capable of modification to accept new, unplanned uses.[17] Thus the solution to the problem is a plan that provides a pedestrian precinct on multiple levels to which individual buildings can be integrated, creating a mega form built by separate developers.

While some skyscrapers are designed for a mixed use with commercial, office, and residential components, they are not designed to be real communities. A major challenge then is to transform them or other large structures into mixed-use communities. The marketplace has been remarkably resistant to this. Malls are a component of an edge city or urban core community but remain firmly committed to be single-use structures. The technical difficulties of a mega form as a community is both a technical construction issue and a design problem. What can be learned from the mega form concept is that large, integrated buildings, envisioned as a whole, is a concept that should not be discarded. The question is whether practical applications can be found. In China or the Gulf oil states, growth is so rapid that the mega form for a small city is now feasible, while it was not fifty or even thirty years ago. These communities are building multiple seventy-story buildings at the same time. This rapid growth is not occurring in the United States, so three complexes—sub-regional centers, edge cities, and transit-oriented development—are the major opportunity areas for the mega form. The waste of land in edge cities—where there are central city concentrations of shopping and employment spread out in auto-urban fashion—seems to make them a logical candidate. With transit hopefully making a comeback in coming decades, the mega form has value for transit-oriented development. Mega forms also have the ability to handle very high densities and at the same time protect natural areas, reduce impervious surfaces to a minimum, and accommodate growth while leaving a minimal carbon footprint. As was the case with the group form, there may also be opportunities at the lower end of the community scale.

Castles are an early example of mega forms, as they housed entire communities, not just military garrisons. In the American Southwest, there is little doubt that the pueblos were freestanding mega form communities. What we think of as the pueblo style, with ladders needed to access entries, may have been a very early settlement pattern. But these are all rather archaic forms.

Figure 4-25. Suburban single-family. Serenbe, Georgia.

Figure 4-26. Schloss Lichtenstein. Swabia, Germany.

Figure 4-27. Cliff dwelling, Mesa Verde National Park. Mesa Verde, Colorado.

Figure 4-28. Taos Pueblo. Taos, New Mexico.

Figure 4-29. Palo Soleri's Arcosanti plan. Near Cordes Junction, Arizona.

Figure 4-30. Town hall, commercial, and library. Saynatsalo, Finland.

Are there some modern examples? A successful mega form on a very small scale is Alvar Aalto's town hall in Saynatsalo, Finland (see figures 4-30 and 4-31). This building has a town hall, town library, shops, and community sauna all in a single structure of unusual beauty. It was envisioned as a single building serving as the core of a small village. It is not hard to envision a larger version with more commercial, offices, and a significant residential component. The materials and design belie the fact that it is a mega structure. The Saynatsalo town hall is important because it demonstrates the concept in familiar and warm materials, as opposed to the space-alien character of Soleri's concept drawing (figure 4-29).[18]

Habitat 67, designed by Moshe Safdie and Associates for the 1967 Montreal World's Fair, is a small, neighborhood-scale mega form (see figure 4-32). This building illustrates the mega structure assembled of standard, prefabricated units stacked together into a single, high-density building. The major difficulty with the prefabrication approach is the cost of design, production, and installation, so that very high volumes are needed. The current growth rates in most American cities will not support the needed scale.

One of the most promising attempts to use a mega structure on a village or neighborhood scale was Manitou Station in New York State. Lee Harris Pomeroy Architects proposed the project in the 1970s as a rail stop and shopping and residential development an hour and ten minutes from downtown Manhattan. If built, it would have constituted a mega form at the village scale in a rural setting, but connected to a metropolitan center by rail. The mega form was a large, V-shaped building with apartments and parking dominating (see figures 4-33 and 4-34). At the intersection of the V was commercial, the train station, and parking. The entire building was surrounded by wooded land and wetlands that were to be left natural. Today, it is understood that this protected land was not only valuable for habitat, but would also have been good for water supply, water quality, storm-water management, and the carbon cycle. Manitou Station would have been a mixed-use community consistent with the current thinking on transit-oriented development. But it never received the zoning approvals necessary for construction. The fearful NIMBYs could not abandon the one-acre, single-family lot mentality, despite what would have been many benefits to the community. The project had a density of only one dwelling unit per acre.

On the West Coast, the Weyerhaeuser headquarters building (figure 4-35) in Washington State provides a contemporary example of a mega structure. The building spans an entire valley, leaving the floodplain and valley floor intact. It shows how such a building can achieve a very high intensity with minimal impact on the landscape by being surrounded with natural areas. While this is a corporate office building, there is no real reason that it could not have been a village with residential, employment, and shopping located on a rail line.

Most major cities and suburbs are carved up by expressways or toll roads that are anywhere from six to ten lanes in width. These divide communities and destroy connectivity, particularly in the suburbs where roads are closed, creating cul-de-sac areas because the cost of building the crossings is so high. In Seattle, both parks and an exposition center cross the main interstate that bisects the city, in what can be considered either a mega form or the structure to accommodate one. There is no reason a mega form similar to the Weyerhaeuser building could not have bridged a depressed road and provide compromise between burying the road, as Boston has done in the Big Dig, and simply leaving the road as a huge void and barrier.

Although we can point to recent examples, much of what we know about the potential of mega structures and mega forms comes from the utopian or unbuilt plans of architects. This goes back to Sant'Ella's Citta Nuova mechanical visions of the city of the future.[19] Paolo Soleri produced an entire book of plans for utopian cities based on mega structures. The Japanese, with land in short supply and an enormous population, developed a number of concept plans—from Kiyonori Kikutake's sketches for a floating city to Kenzo Tange's plan for the expansion of Tokyo into Tokyo Bay with a series of connected mega structures. Many of these utopian plans were so large scale that they had little hope of ever being adopted as a model. But the concept cannot be dismissed out of hand simply because these architects' visions exceeded reality. It clearly has potential value today for urban cores, transit-oriented development, and some small-scale communities.

Figure 4-31. Stairs to town hall level. Saynatsalo, Finland.

Figure 4-32. Precast, modular mega structure. Habitat 67, Montreal, Canada.

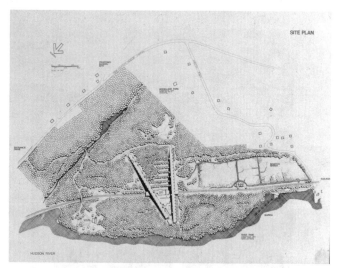

Figure 4-33. Plan drawing for Manitou Station, Garrison, New York, by Lee Harris Pomeroy Architects.

Figure 4-34. Perspective of model for Manitou Station, by Lee Harris Pomeroy Associates.

Figure 4-35. Weyerhaeuser headquarters building. King County, Washington.

Design with Mega Forms

Making a true mega form is very difficult. There are pure design issues and there is the question about what is appropriate for mega form communities. Paolo Soleri advocated large-scale communities, small and large cities, and even metropolitan areas that would be a single structure. This requires a level of planning that is beyond the realm of feasibility. At the small end of the community scale, mega forms become a feasible building that can be conceived as a single structure (e.g., the Saynatsalo town hall) or group of connected structures.

Many buildings that are built today are larger than the historical mega forms. The modern skyscraper and regional malls are both mega-structure-scaled buildings. But these structures are simply big buildings for a single use—a true mega form is a community with living, shopping, and employment integrated into a single structure. Shopping malls undergoing major refits are generally mixed-use developments in either compositional or group form configurations with multiple buildings, not mega forms. With rare exceptions, the malls do not make the connection to other land uses in the community. The skyscraper in scale is a mega structure and could be designed to include residential. Unfortunately, it is treated like a building to be placed on a lot or block in a compositional form.

The edge city is a regional employment and shopping node. While the street and land use patterns structure these areas, they are not really planned for that purpose. Market forces dictated the concentration of uses, and the result was a mix of auto-urban commercial with office buildings laid over a preexisting street pattern. Since edge cities take decades to develop, how does one impose the needed design control to create a community in a single structure?

The edge city has the core element of a mega form in the regional mall. There are generally strips of commercial that form around or precede the mall, taking advantage of the traffic it generates. In Schaumburg, Illinois, there are two malls, a power center, and a number of big box and category killer uses (bookstores and clothing) on three adjoining blocks. It does not take a rocket scientist to see that these could be linked together into a single, pedestrian-oriented mega form. Offices and hotels in the area could easily be integrated into the form as well. Using parking structures, rather than at-grade parking, frees the space needed to concentrate these uses along a pedestrian precinct.

While typically much smaller than an edge city, a transit-oriented development would use the same principles. The transit stop would be within the structure that would provide mixed residential, commercial, and office space. Parking garages would be built into the building to accommodate people driving to the train station. A grade-separated pedestrian precinct would ensure that neither roads nor the train tracks represented a barrier to movement.

Planning for Community Form

Society would be richer if all three community forms were used. Developers and municipalities would have additional options for creating a distinct identity. But the default form in the United States, compositional form, is very poorly used, even at the neighborhood scale. The group form is acceptable for small, new communities in the countryside, small developments in environmentally sensitive areas, or the neighborhood scale. New hamlets and villages are ideal for this. Planners need to reclaim the neighborhood and reassess the appropriate form of development to give these areas greater identity. The transit-oriented development and urban cores provide an opportunity to use mega forms.

REGIONAL AND METROPOLITAN FORM

Metropolitan areas are very large, comprising numerous municipalities, counties, and in some cases several states. They are growing without any serious regional planning. There are three reasons for a regional form: to create an intelligible regional community, to guide transportation, and to preserve some rural areas within the region. Except for the central cities, almost all the nations' metropolitan regions have a terrible sameness and interchangeability. A metropolitan form with unique character would address this.

Having a plan for the metropolitan form is critical for placing densities where they can be served by transit, and for guiding expansion to maximize the effectiveness of the land use and transportation system. As metropolitan areas continue to grow, and grow together, the need for some rural area simply to provide visual relief is important. Sustainability suggests crops grown close to the market, so this is an additional rationale for rural land within the metropolitan area. In many metropolitan areas growth is spreading into some of the best farmland, which ultimately may mean having to open up less productive areas. With a very broad brush, there is a need to deal with the character of our communities on a regional scale, and the metropolitan form is an important tool.

There are three types of regions: rural, independent, and metropolitan. The economy of the rural region is largely agricultural. Much of the central and northern plains and parts of the mountain states fall into this pattern, with little industry other than agriculture, timber, or resource extraction. At the other end of the scale are metropolitan areas surrounding business and industrial cities, or even merging into a megalopolis, as from Boston through Washington, D.C., and other areas of the nation. In between these extremes are communities that are only partially dependent on agriculture, and have a series of towns and small cities that have well-established industrial or other nonagricultural-related businesses. These are the independent regions that have a mixed economy and no large metropolitan area. For the most part, most residents of independent regions work close to home and do not commute to a metropolitan region. Some of these independent regions will be tourist destinations, with economies based on tourist and vacation homes.

The planning issue with rural and independent regional forms is retaining the freestanding community character by avoiding sprawl, which degrades the character of the community even when there is no threat of becoming a composite community. If municipalities and counties worked together and planned in a sustainable manner, it would be possible to deal with the issue by having counties provide for rural areas and concentrate sub-urban and urban development in municipalities. The threat of being a composite community is often greatest in tourist areas, where every rural landowner wants a piece of the action and sprawl is extreme along major roads.

The metropolitan region's long-term growth makes it important to find a mechanism to permanently internalize rural areas within its boundaries. Currently, metropolitan regions and metropolises are simply growing outward and freestanding communities are being absorbed. Even regions or counties with growth management plans for the most part are treating rural areas as short-term holding zones. In metropolitan regions and some cities in independent regions, there needs to be a plan for long-term development and preservation.

There are five basic forms that could serve as models for metropolitan areas to guide growth over a long time period as an alternative to the continual sprawl into rural areas. Four are geometric: greenbelt, star, linear, and satellite. The fifth is organic, and is dictated by physical features such as stream corridors or topography. All these plans have a role for rural as well as sub-urban and urban character types within the metropolitan planning area. The current do-nothing approach creates a formless, growing blob that spreads over everything. It is an expanding sheet with commercial strips extending along all major arterial roads, filled with a mix of predominantly suburban, auto-urban, and estate character types with no rational pattern basis. It is the default, however, because regional planning agencies have failed to convince their constituent municipalities to

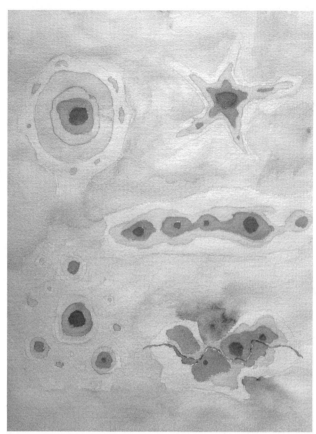

Figure 4-36. Metropolitan forms: greenbelt, star, linear, satellite, organic.

work within a regional framework. All five model forms described below and shown in figure 4-36 need to be considered as alternatives for metropolitan planning.

Greenbelt

A greenbelt is a rural area that contains a metropolitan area within a permanent rural boundary, rather than an urban growth boundary that can be expanded. The greenbelt model is one of the oldest forms, dating back to the "city beautiful" and "garden cities" movements in the latter part of the nineteenth century. The vision of these movements was a major city that grew to a fixed size with additional garden cities built around it. This form delimits the central city (possibly including inner suburbs) to a fixed size. This is the most rigorous of forms because once a greenbelt is established the city's area is limited. It is likely that development beyond the greenbelt will be in another jurisdiction. The core city and its suburbs must accept the notion of a maximum size. It places a great deal more pressure on the community to grow by redevelopment and intensified densities over time. In Howard's garden city, the greenbelt was not a belt at all, but a ring of garden cities surrounding the central city.[20] In Ottawa, Canada, the greenbelt is just that, a belt that remains rural. Unfortunately, outside the belt a development pattern remarkably similar to that inside the greenbelt is developing, rather than a series of additional freestanding or greenbelt communities.

What happens beyond the greenbelt? The answer has not yet been determined. Should there then be a satellite pattern so that smaller greenbelt communities would be the form of growth as the central area reached capacity? Raymond Unwin's sketches seem to imply that beyond the central city there was a generally rural area with a satellite pattern of freestanding towns.[21] One alternative pattern might be series of alternating rings—urbanized, rural, urbanized, rural—like an archery target, as shown in the upper left of figure 4-36. Both the satellite or ring patterns would rely on a circumferential transit system in addition to the radial system to service the outlying communities. The circular transit route is the most effective routing system.

Star

The star (upper right of figure 4-36) is a radial pattern with arms extending out from the central core, and rural lands that can be retained between the star's arms. Rail lines establish logical radials that represent a natural basis for the plan. As these are fixed facilities that were generally established in the nineteenth century, radiating out from a city, it was a logical form for a regional plan. It can be found in the rail suburbs around many cities; Chicago, New York, and Philadelphia had systems of rail and interurban service well out into rural areas. While other cities, such as Washington, D.C., had regional plans calling for such a form, these died with the interstate system, which not only encouraged highways but also funded major arterial improvements that enabled communities to expand into the spaces between the rail corridors, thereby dooming the regional plan.

The star needs a strongly radial transit system. It works less well with a radial highway system because the densities are lower, which reduces the amount of rural land that can be retained. The other major disadvantage of the radial road system is that it is hugely expensive to expand capacity as development goes further and further away from the central city, which can be done only by adding lanes to the roads. It is far easier to add capacity to rail transit.

Circumferential roads must be limited to minor routes that cannot carry high volumes. At some point the arms become too far apart to permit easy travel from one to another. This may be where a major node is needed on the arm; at this point a circumferential rail line is appropriate, and an intermediate arm might be started or an existing arm be split into two.

Linear

The linear form (center right of figure 4-36) is unique in that it extends primarily in one dimension, either because of natural constraints—such as a river, lake, or ocean—or some other difficulty in moving in other directions. For example, southern Florida's eastern coast, with the ocean and everglades on either side, is a sprawling strip of formerly freestanding communities that have grown together and expanded westward as far as they

Figure 4-37. Linear city served by monorail. Wuppertal, Germany.

Figure 4-38. Monorail over river. Wuppertal, Germany.

could. The major reason for the linear form was transportation. Soria y Mata's Ciudad Lineal was a direct result of experience building Madrid's first rail line.[22] Radial rail lines are inefficient because the travel is primarily one way, into the city in the morning and out in the evening, with less travel at midday. Transit is most efficient in serving a series of destinations in a single line so that people are getting on and off in most stations evenly during the day. In the city of Wuppertal, Germany (see figures 4-37 and 4-38), a linear city developed along a river with numerous factories and other uses nearby. A monorail straddles the river serving the city. The river valley contains the linear city, and because jobs, homes, and shopping are scattered along the length of the line, the system has continuous request service.

In this pattern the rural would be linear and restrict growth to a corridor where transit was being provided by a series of parallel lines. In the 1950s the northern lakeshore suburbs of Chicago were served by three heavy rail lines spaced about a mile apart, serving suburbs with centers on the rail corridor. In this development form, parallel rail corridors, each separated by a mile, would enable transit to serve nearly all work trips as well as many other trips. One additional requirement would be regular transfers between the rail lines so that the parallel corridors were effectively interconnected. Truck roads would be linear, but freeways would be undesirable.

Satellite

The satellite pattern (lower left of figure 4-36) is where the major urban area is surrounded by smaller-scale communities, all of which are freestanding. Thus a large city would have as satellites a few small cities and a great many towns and villages. The satellite was the pattern of settlement in Europe and the United States in the nineteenth century, when most communities were freestanding. It was the natural pattern of urbanization when most people lived in rural areas in order to provide the needed food and fiber. The hamlet was the base community—a few grew to villages and fewer yet to towns and cities. The increased level of specialization meant that the higher level serviced a number of lower-level communities.

The pattern, while not perfectly regular, was influenced by locational advantages for trade or industry that allowed some communities to grow much larger. It is a free form, with rural land dominating and separating the communities. It will have a full range of freestanding hamlets, villages, towns, and cities. This is the pattern of rural regions and most of the area in independent regions. This pattern cannot easily be served with transit. At best, a system where the larger freestanding communities were organized in a starlike pattern is feasible. Sir Raymond Unwin's 1929 plans for London envisioned a series of satellites around the central city. They were to be served by transit and roads, and the green spaces would have eliminated the highway strips or ribbons.[23]

In theory, the growth is accommodated by ever more new garden cities, which would be ever further out from the central city. If the communities are all to remain freestanding, this would seem to create a problem for long-term growth. The element that is critical is the formula, which would not only have to address the mix and spacing for hamlets, villages, towns, or cities, but would also have to plan for whether communities could grow to new levels. The rules would also have to determine where some communities would be able to grow together to create a composite form. Ideally the mix, growth, and merger rules would be in place from the beginning of the metropolitan plan. Only a few areas would be programmed to grow together to create a larger composite community (see chapter 2 regarding freestanding communities and spacing standards).

Organic

In some regions there will be physical features that strongly suggest the areas within the metropolitan area to remain rural. This is the organic form (lower right of figure 4-36), and is likely to be the result of a modification of any of the other forms. The distinguishing feature is that the natural or agricultural areas would force a major modification of the geometric form. Stream or river corridors and major topographic features are the most obvious. The San Francisco metropolitan area is a great example of a region whose form is shaped by natural features. While there are some metropolitan areas where natural features by necessity dictate the regional form, it is desirable to consider these natural features to assist in shaping any of the other forms. Floodplains should be agricultural or natural, while rugged terrain suggests natural or countryside. Prime farmland represents another way to identify areas that should be rural. The arterial road network should avoid these areas, leaving only rural roads. Rail can go through these areas without stopping, so it is not a threat to rural spaces.

The Blob or Sheet (the Status Quo)

Many regions have no regional plan other than a composite of municipal land use plans. Even where one or more counties are attempting to do growth management, the result at best is a moving urban-growth boundary and formless metropolitan region with strips running for miles. While small cities may get away with this, the metropolis and large cities need to have a planned form as they continue to grow. As mentioned above, the eastern coast of Florida is a sheet extending from south of Miami to the northern end of Palm Beach County. The twenty-year county plan typically calls for rural areas to be preserved, but as the plans are revised every five years, the boundary moves out and ultimately the rural areas disappear. Freestanding communities are not protected and the rural area will be lost, often more rapidly than the metropolitan area is growing.

The need for metropolitan regions to have a plan is important to effective transportation or economic planning. Today, most of the metropolitan areas seem to be similar and often justify being called slurbs. It is important to municipal identity to have a plan because that promotes a context for each municipality and improves the perceived quality of the region. It is important that municipalities work together to strengthen and support regional form planning. In the end, each community would benefit from having a clear place within the region and from a breakup of the auto-urban strips that now dominate metropolitan forms.

The rural and independent regions currently have a satellite pattern that reflects their historical development. The spacing will depend on the type of agricultural economy, with farm or ranch size dictating market areas for communities because it sets the rural population density. Only the larger communities in these two regions will have need for a metropolitan planning strategy.

CONCLUSION

The form that designers use in building their development or neighborhood should be tackled using all the various approaches. This is most true for small, freestanding settlements. Municipalities or developers of new communities need to consider the use of different forms to distinguish neighborhoods. Edge cities and transit-oriented development are naturals for the use of mega forms. The use of all three forms, rather than just the compositional form, would enrich by creating communities with greater identities, in part from their form. At the regional scale, the profession that considered this form of planning in the 1950s and 1960s has largely given up attempting to provide metropolitan areas a form that preserves any rural areas; successive regional plans just continue the existing pattern, creating one giant slurb (see chapter 1). The result is that freestanding communities are swallowed up one after the other as the region grows and expands. The goal of preserving rural areas found in many comprehensive plans is just an illusion, as each successive twenty-year plan expands into the rural surroundings. Both community and regional forms need to be used by planners.

CHAPTER 5

Community Character Measurement

One of the key objectives of the community character system is for planners, designers, and residents to have a common vocabulary to more easily and reliably communicate about replicating or retaining community character. Terms like "rural" and "small town" are often used in describing communities that have in fact lost those values. Measuring character is important because these words may take on a very different meaning to an individual living in a large city, a suburb, or on a farm. This difference becomes more troubling if the individual is making a decision on local regulations. In this chapter, methods for the measurement of community character are set forth. All these methods are objective measures that can be replicated. The ability to quantify character makes it a better planning tool than subjective characterizations.

Classifying and measuring on a continuum divided into a limited number of categories creates a problem. When a continuum is divided into six or eight categories, it suggests dramatic changes at specific points. Only one well-known continua that exhibits this characteristic—the temperature of water, where specific points correspond to the conversion from solid to liquid and liquid to gas. The nature of most continua is that a minimal change occurs at every point along its length. Community scale is measured in population or dwelling units. The question is: when does a village become a town? A change of one person or one dwelling unit does not effect that change. There is a point where the village starts to get too large but is still too small to function like a town. The solution is to have gaps in the continuum to reflect the transition from one category to another. Similarly, there is a gradual change from rural to sub-urban classes, as well as between different character types. For state, scale, or character type (chapters 2 and 3) there exists a continuum from

Figure 5-1. Freestanding village surrounded by open land. Swabia, Germany.

Figure 5-2. View to center of city. Schwerte, Germany.

Figure 5-3. View to suburb separated by green space. Schwerte, Germany.

the smallest to largest and from most rural to most urban, and gaps are specifically provided for these transitions. Current zoning often has many transitional residential zoning categories, which makes it difficult to determine if a proposed development will change the character of an area.

COMMUNITY STATE AND SCALE

There are only two community states—freestanding and composite. To be freestanding, a community must be physically separated from the next community by a rural or natural environment (see figure 5-1). This represents a real challenge for measuring existing character because it is not always clear at what point two communities merge and become a composite community. It is obvious that long before subdivisions or uses in the two communities abut, they are too close together to really be freestanding, even though there may be some rural or vacant land between them. Because development can occur both inside and outside municipal limits, and because of the possibility of annexation to another community, it is best to set a specific distance between communities as a goal. In general, a separation of five miles can be used. Looking at a good map of the state or region, one finds this spacing quite common.[1] This distance needs to be field verified to ensure that is has not been reduced by sprawl. Similarly, a lower distance is possible when there are firm land use controls, as in Europe, where there are very hard edges enforced by the region. Figures 5-2 and 5-3 show a separation of about three miles with no intervening development between a suburb and city center in Germany, where spacing is tighter.

A second measurement is the ratio of rural land to total area of the settlement, which should be greater than 0.95, based on the five-mile distance between two settlements. The ratio basis provides a little more flexibility and better deals with the problem of sprawling development beyond municipal boundaries. It is less effective if the municipality has permitted linear growth along major roads.

Community scale is a numerical continuum that uses population or dwelling units as a base. Table 2-1 in chapter 2 provides the measurements for each community. There are significant gaps between scale levels that account for the transition. If a community falls in the gap, the planners should provide text noting that it is in transition from one scale to the next.

MEASURING COMMUNITY CHARACTER

There are a number of approaches to measuring community character, but not all measurements are universally applicable across the entire continuum. Some measurements are of primary value to one character class. The most universal of the measures is the *community character diagram*. This tool has the ability to measure current character, and at the same time is useful in predicting future character by projection techniques or by analyzing plans or zoning.

Volume measures (building, landscape, and site volume ratios) also have wide application to measuring community character because they explain urban core to estate very well, though they are not very useful in rural character types. They are also excellent for the understanding of small-scale problems, like the too-big house (McMansions and starter castles).

In the urban class, the *D/H ratio* (distance divided by height) measurement is very important in differentiating the three types; it is also valuable in defining rural spatial types. The *figure-ground* is a visual analysis technique that is often useful as well.

Community Character Diagram

A community character diagram is both a planning and a management tool. It can be used to identify the character of an area or municipality by measuring the percentages of land in different community character types, from urban to rural. It is able to predict future character from a land use plan or zoning ordinance and can help to manage changes.

The community character diagram is used for plotting community character from measurements of land uses taken from maps or aerial photographs. It also easily plots existing character and allows for easy projection of future character. Thus it is the most universal analytic tool used to quantify community character. The scale is a triangular diagram,[2] which permits data on three different characteristics to be measured and displayed in a graphic form. In this case, the diagram requires the recording of the mix of three different classes of community character: urban, sub-urban, and rural. Superimposed over the basic triangular diagram are additional lines that indicate the range of character types. The face of the diagram contains the five classifications: agriculture/natural, countryside, estate, suburban, and urban types (see figure 5-4). Agriculture and natural are merged because land cover, not development scale, is the distinguishing factor. The urban class is not broken up on the diagram because there are other criteria that distinguish between them. The measurement is done by class—urban, sub-urban, and rural—because there is no easy method to plot six different variables. There are some rules that need to be applied for estate, vacant land, parks, and some specific uses.

Each point on the diagram represents a specific, unique mix of the three character classes. Each of the corners of the triangle represents pure character. The top of the diagram repre-

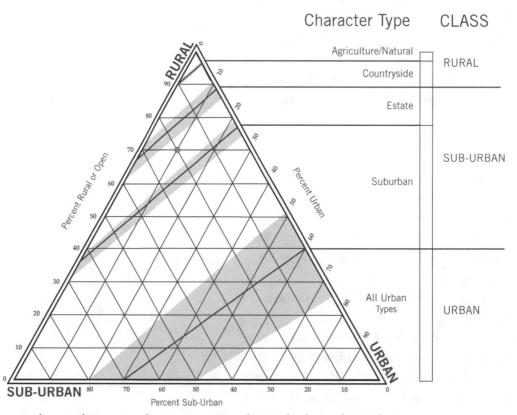

Figure 5-4. Community character diagram. Dot shows an area 70% rural, 20% sub-urban, and 10% urban.

sents an area that is 100 percent rural; the lower left corner, an area that is 100 percent sub-urban; and the lower right, 100 percent urban. To use the community character diagram one needs information on the percentage of land in each of the three character classes, which can be measured from maps or aerial photographs. There is a 10 percent grid over the triangle to assist in plotting character. The triangle is divided into areas indicating five of the eight types. Natural and agriculture are combined because they are distinguished by land cover or use rather than the amount of developed land. Both estate and suburban are shown. Only urban is shown because the degree of enclosure, rather than open space versus developed land, is the critical variable between the various urban classes. Once the location is plotted, it appears within one of the bands representing the character types. The target for any character type should be the middle of the range in character, along the centerline of the character type on the diagram. Using the centerlines provides maximum separation between character types, which is important for maintaining distinctions in character. This makes it a useful descriptive tool.

Figure 5-5 is an aerial photo of a portion of Amarillo, Texas. By measuring the percent of the area occupied by each of the types, one can plot the existing character. The classification will result in a map similar to a land use map, except that it has the three character types (see figure 5-6) instead of land uses.

Figure 5-5. Aerial photo used as base for character mapping. Amarillo, Texas.

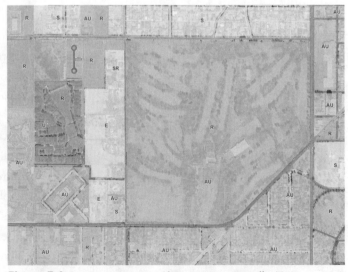

Figure 5-6. Existing community character map. Amarillo, Texas.

Once the existing character is plotted on the chart, the community character diagram can be used in a variety of planning-related tasks. As with land use plans, the first step is the classification of an area's character at the start of the land use study or zoning-change analysis. In the case of Amarillo (figures 5-5 and 5-6), the area is 18 percent urban, 33 percent suburban, and 49 percent open space and rural. Only 4 percent is vacant, so the character has limited potential to change. Second, if one has access to historical aerial photographs, the changes in character over time can be plotted. Third, the diagram permits the forecasting of future land use by trend or zoning. Lastly, the diagram may be used to develop the zoning needed to achieve a desired future community character.

Planning involves determining the impact of future development. Perhaps the most valuable element of the community character diagram is its ability to evaluate proposals and predict the future character of an area based on the input. The diagram may be used in two different ways to achieve this: to plot trends or to evaluate a specific plan or zoning amendment. Clearly, if aerial photographs or past land use maps of a town or area over a period of time were available, its character could be plotted at various points in its history. Like any graph, it would then be possible to make estimates as to where that trend of development might lead. This sort of trend analysis permits both straight-line and curving trends (see figure 5-7, below) to be estimated on the same basis as with other graphs. The straight line connecting the earliest and latest points or fitted to the trend on the diagram will produce a straight line for the entire history. If the points show a steady change over time, then a curved-line projection may make more sense. Predictions based on trends are reliable only to the degree that future development follows past trends.

Unlike other forms of graphs, the triangular diagram is not dependent on trend analysis for its predictive powers. It can take input from a land use plan or zoning map and provide a definitive prediction of the future character that would result from following that plan or ordinance. While this is not tied to time, its real value is that it lets the citizens and officials precisely understand the impact of the plan or zoning. The impact of several proposed developments on the future character of an area

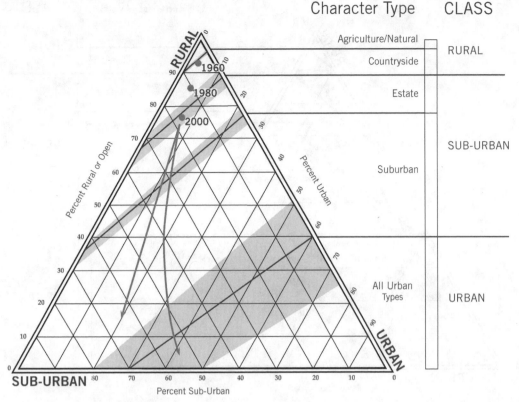

Figure 5-7. Plotting past character of a community and projecting future character.

may also be predicted. The ability to predict changes in the ultimate future character is particularly important if the proposed developments vary from the plan or ordinance on which the projected future character was based.

There is a third way to use the community character diagram to assist the community in reaching agreement on its desired future character. Starting at the existing character there are a limited number of possible futures; they are limited to all-sub-urban development or all-urban development. Plotting the possible futures is then easy. A line parallel to the left side of the triangle is the projection of sub-urban development, as shown by the arrow. A line parallel to the right side projects urban development, which results in another triangle (in gray on figure 5-8) that contains all possible options for development, urban or suburban.

For example, if 15 percent of the rural or vacant land in an area is converted to suburban, our plot moves down the

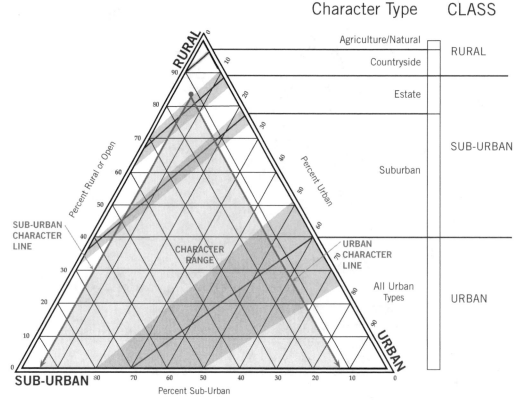

Figure 5-8. Possible future character options, suburban or urban.

diagram parallel to the left side of the diagram, with a 15 percent reduction in rural area and a corresponding increase in the amount of suburban land. If it were converted to urban, the direction of movement would parallel the right side of the diagram. It is possible then to block out all existing land uses and plot the results of a build-out using either the existing plan or the zoning ordinance. It is often the case that the analysis of a plan and an ordinance do not produce the same result.

Predicting future character based on existing plans or ordinances is useful for officials and the public, as it informs better than a map what the community will be like twenty years hence. In some cases, particularly with existing county zoning, the community may be shocked at the results.[3] The community character diagram thus might show an enormous shift in character. Ideally, municipalities would have a build-out projection to their ultimate boundaries. The build-out projections are likely to show a different picture than a twenty-year growth projection. Their value in educating the population about the im-

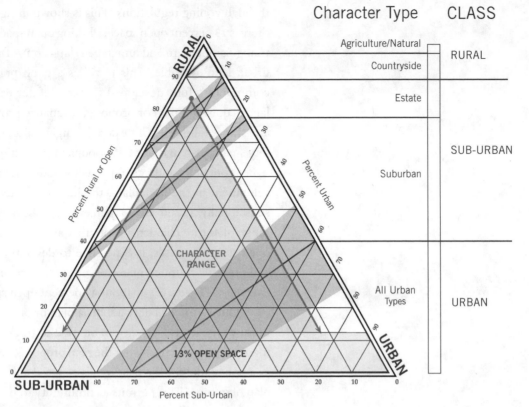

Figure 5-9. Using open space to define character.

pact of zoning or open space acquisition plans is an important use of the community character diagram. There are computer tools that make this far easier. Geographic information systems can all provide the data inputs for the triangles. The character system has been or can be integrated into other software programs—such as SAVES (integrated) and CommunityViz (it is uncertain whether this can be integrated)[4]—that allow the planner to fully evaluate alternatives or to assist in developing them.

The community character diagram also accounts for open space, parks, rural uses, or unbuildable land, all of which can be considered as undeveloped on the diagram. Land that is permanently preserved as open space or a park is permanent rural land for the purposes of the triangle analysis. Unbuildable land, such as floodplains or wetlands that remain open, also remains rural in character. The percentage of unbuildable land represents a floor to the future character triangle, where the amount of undevelopable or preserved land is plotted along the bottom of the diagram. A municipality can plan to preserve land as parks or through zoning regulations. This is shown in figure 5-9, where there is 13 percent open space. Plotting open space truncates the triangular diagram and limits the relative mix of urban and suburban land available. This provides a good prediction of the community's fully developed character if, for example, a parkland acquisition plan or proposed ordinance protecting natural areas were followed. This example might represent the community's park plan and normal floodplain protection.[5] If the ordinance contains standards to protect woodlands and prohibit development in the floodplain, the level of protection might be substantially raised to 26 percent, significantly altering the range of future character. Note that as permanently preserved open space increases, it is possible to develop urban buildings and preserve so much open space that the area has a suburban character. This occurs at about 47 percent open space.

Once a municipality adopts a plan or ordinance the community character diagram can be used to track actual development over time against what the plan proposes. Again it is useful as a policy tool for the testing of proposed amendments to the plan or zoning. This permits a community to better manage its decision making with regard to community character. In a built-up community where there is little undeveloped land, the triangle would show a shift from one character type to another, moving the character parallel to the bottom of the chart.

In developing a comprehensive plan, the community is asked to decide the type of character it wants to achieve at maturity or build-out. Figure 5-10 shows an example of a community that wants its future character to be suburban. As indicated previously, the target should be in the center of the suburban zone so that there is clear separation between the adjoining character types, avoiding transition areas. In figure 5-10 the midpoint of suburban is used as the cutoff creating a triangle. The minimum open space preservation (28 percent was assumed in the illustration, but the municipal plan would provide the actual number) cuts off a small portion of the suburban area, leaving a four-sided shape as the range of development potential that will produce the desired character. Any location along the bottom line of the shape produces the desired character. The critical element is to have sufficient open space preserved to achieve the desired character, depending on whether one chooses suburban, urban, or some mix of the two. As a higher percentage of the development is urban, more open space is required to ensure the desired character. The bottom line then represents a way to set the zoning specifications. The use of fifteen-thousand-square-foot lots would follow the left-hand border. A cluster development having 40 percent open space and using ten-thousand-square-foot lots intersects the bottom of the options. A planned development using all urban dwelling unit types would have to provide 56 percent open space.

The question may come up as to whether the desired character is possible. In figure 5-10 the existing character is very close to the transition from countryside to estate. If the community is just beginning to plan using character, it is will be difficult to achieve an estate character because the area would have to preserve between 65 and 75 percent of the community in open space—and since the community was already 22 percent developed, actual open space for new development would need to be between 83 and 96 percent. The closer the existing

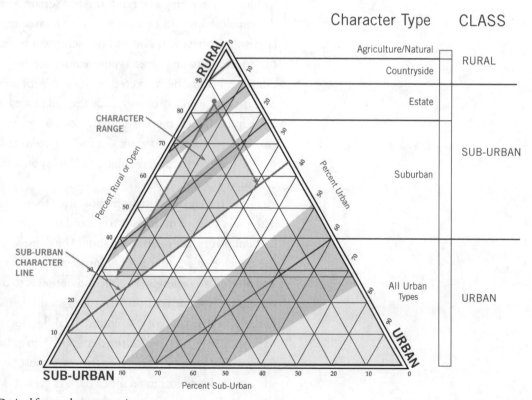

Figure 5-10. Desired future character options.

character is to the desired character, the more extreme the clustering or acquisition program needed to achieve the desired character will be.

Rules for Plotting Existing Land Use

Rural

Agriculture, forest, vacant, or open spaces (including golf courses and parks) are all classed as rural. Residential lots of twenty acres or more should be shown as one-acre sub-urban and the rest rural. Vacant land is borrowed open space and so is classified as rural, even though other character types may surround it.

Sub-urban

There are different rules for each of the two sub-urban types, suburban and estate. Single-family residential of fifteen- to twenty-thousand-square-foot lots are the average for suburban lots, with a range of ten thousand square feet representing the smallest and lots of nearly an acre in area representing the largest. Lots between one and ten acres will be estate. Because the community character type provides for only three classes, estate areas must be corrected. It is possible for an area to be 100 percent estate, but if one extends the estate area it runs off the left-hand edge of the triangle at about 53 percent vacant. To compensate on the diagram, lots with two to ten acres should have a one- to three-acre area coded as suburban and the rest classified as rural.

Where cluster development is used there are two options. The most precise method is to record the development in constituent pieces; the open space should be considered as rural and the developed portion as the appropriate urban or sub-urban and plotted accordingly. The second option is to determine that the cluster is suburban using the triangle and then recording it as entirely in that category. A commercial development or office park with 50–60 percent of the developed site in landscaped surfaces would be suburban. Note that care must be taken to classify undeveloped lots in an office park as vacant. Many small institutional uses, as well as schools with their playing fields, should be considered suburban.

Urban

The three urban types—urban, auto-urban, and urban core—will be more fully covered in the companion volume, *A Guide to Planning for Community Character*. Nearly all commercial, office, industrial, and other nonresidential uses are classed as urban. The distinction between them is not the amount of vacant land or parks, as was true with suburban types, as there are areas of all three types provide no open space. Auto-urban will be the classification of strip development, whether in city or suburb, by virtue of the large areas of parking lots. The older downtowns with buildings to the sidewalk line are generally urban. The classification needs to account for total area in off-street parking lots. Any area with 50 percent surface parking is auto-urban. Urban core is distinguished from urban by the presence of buildings over ten stories high.

Nearly all residential on lots of fewer than ten thousand square feet will be one of the urban types. Alleys allow small single-family and attached single-family lots to be urban. Without an alley, those lots will be auto-urban, because the street face will be a parking lot or driveway that occupies much of the front yard. Low-density, multi-family residential is likely to be auto-urban and will have surface parking lots. Urban parking will be in structures or below the units. Only when buildings exceed ten to fifteen stories would urban core be considered.

In the existing community character map of Amarillo in figure 5-6 (page 143), each of the character types has been shown and then measured to determine area, which is then converted to a percentage and plotted on the diagram. The area is 96 percent developed, with only 4 percent vacant land.

The existing land use in almost every community has many areas where the residential development lies in the transition. Is it urban or auto-urban or suburban? There are other cases where the question is whether it is suburban or estate. This is one of the reasons why having a community-character-based plan and ordinance is important, because with community character no developments would be built that are unclear or transitional in character. The zoning would produce neighborhoods that were clearly one character type or another.

Determining whether to map an area as countryside or agricultural can be difficult. Often this is an area of farmland with scattered one- to five-acre lots stripped along the road, and is further confused by homes on lots of ten to forty acres. There are two choices. The first is to map lots as suburban and home-sites on the larger parcels as suburban, and if the area is countryside on the community character triangle, then map it as countryside. This requires determining the area to be measured in advance. The second method is less precise, but areas of scattered subdivisions and agricultural land can sometimes be evaluated visually. The application of the triangle and mapping of house lots is particularly important because it makes for accurate dwelling unit and population counts.

Forest cover and maturity will also be a factor. A new subdivision on lots of one acre or more built in a cornfield will look very suburban, with large houses and little landscaping. The same subdivision built in a forested area is nearly invisible from the road, and here estate is the obvious choice. An older subdivision with mature landscaping will also look very different from the new one. In most cases one should classify the new subdivisions as if the trees were mature, unless there is little landscaping being done. Landscape or forest cover is important enough so that slight adjustments in the break points between character types should be made—a little more urban for a lack of landscaping, a bit more rural where there is heavy forest cover or very intense landscaping.

VOLUME RATIOS

The three volume ratios—building, landscape, and site—identified in chapter 1 represent another way to evaluate the character of an area or use. The first volume measure is the building volume ratio (BVR). This measures the three-dimensional mass of a building and compares it to the area of a site. The second, landscape volume ratio (LVR), compares the mass of landscape to the area of a site. The third measure, site volume ratio (SVR), combines the first two. The site volume ratio is the landscape volume ratio minus the building volume ratio. Any site with more landscape volume than building volume has a positive value. Where the building volume is larger than the landscape volume, then the site volume ratio is negative.

Figure 5-11a. Two-acre forested estate character, high SVR. Pierce Township, Ohio.

Figure 5-11b. Two-acre lots in open field, suburban character, low SVR. Long Grove, Illinois.

As a tool, the volume measures are more easily adapted to micro-scale situations than is the community character diagram. Volume tools clearly explain differences between character types. Enclosed urban spaces will typically have large negative site volume ratios and sub-urban environments will have positive values, reflecting their garden-like quality. In figures 5-11a and 5-11b, the density and lot sizes are identical (one-acre lots), but in figure 5-11a the SVR is very strongly positive because the homes were built in a mature woodland with minimal clearing, so the landscape volume is many times the building volume. Mature forest with a tree canopy fifty feet in height results in an LVR approaching 5.0. In the homes built in an old farm field in figure 5-11b, the LVR of the grasses is 0.2. Thus, with similar BVR values on both sites (approximately 0.05), the SVR values are 4.95 and 0.15, respectively. This explains the estate character of figure 5.11a, while figure 5.11b is nearly suburban in character despite the large lots.

Typical measures of intensity, density, floor area ratios (FAR), building coverage, or even open space ratios do not thoroughly describe the character of a building lot or development. A one-story automated warehouse with a FAR identical to a one-story office building can have a BVR three times as large. The BVR of urban core, urban, and auto-urban areas are also predictably different, and like D/H it can be used to distinguish between these types. Thus, from urban core to estate, the volume measures are important, while they are far less so for rural types.

The landscape volume is totally related to land cover, and thus has an extreme range of LVR values from near zero for desert or short-grass prairie land covers to more than ten in the forests of the Pacific Northwest. As a result, the SVR numbers indicate the land cover but do not define the rural character type.

In using SVR, recognize that trees grow. A development with newly planted trees will have its character dominated by buildings. The SVR increases in value as the trees grow and begin to dominate. The classic suburban neighborhoods and the most desirable urban, single-family, residential neighborhoods will have trees that arch over the buildings and streets. Vegetation gets a high rating in community-preference surveys. But such areas are generally over fifty years old, very different from, say, a brand-new development built in what was a farm field. It is unfair to compare a new development with very young trees to an older one with mature trees. New Urbanists often show pairs of slides contrasting an urban neighborhood with mature trees (figure 5-12a) and a new suburban neighborhood with only a few, small trees (figure 5-12b). This is not a legitimate comparison of the two character types. The game could be played the other way, showing a new urban neighborhood (figure 5-13a) against a suburban one with large, mature street trees (figure 5-13b). The volume measures indicate that it is the landscape volume of the mature trees that is the critical factor. Figures 5-14a and 5-14b present a fair comparison of urban homes with either young or mature trees. The importance of trees to the character of all urban and sub-urban types is undeniable. In ad-

Figure 5-12a. Well-landscaped urban character. Boston, Massachusetts.

Figure 5-12b. Poorly landscaped new suburb with auto-urban character. Dubuque, Iowa.

Figure 5-13a. Poorly landscaped urban with negative SVR. Denver, Colorado.

Figure 5-13b. More desirable, lushly landscaped suburban with a high, positive SVR. Savannah, Georgia.

Figure 5-14a. Large, negative SVR; less desirable. Denver, Colorado.

Figure 5-14b. Mature trees improve SVR and desirability. Doylestown, Pennsylvania.

dition to their aesthetic quality, they provide animal habitat, shade, and natural cooling.

The volume measures are also important to the concern about the too-big house or teardown. The "monster" houses (McMansions) have become a problem in many communities in suburbs built between the late 1940s and early 1960s. The original, modest homes were typically ranches, Cape Cods, or small, two-story boxes with eight-foot ceilings throughout and shallow roof pitches of five in twelve.[6] The average size of a home has doubled since then, which has an impact in terms of the environment and community character. Figure 5-15a shows the standard home from the early 1950s on a 10,000 square-foot lot.

Figure 5-15a. Small home and small lot, low BVR. Libertyville, Illinois.

Figure 5-15b. Very large home on small lot; very high BVR will change character. Vernon Hills, Illinois.

Table 5-1. Incremental changes in building volume ratio from changes in building design

Element changed	Starting condition	Changed condition	BVR	Percentage increase
Floor area	1,200 sq. ft.	none	0.150	0
Ceiling height	8 ft.	10 ft.	0.174	16
Vaulted ceiling	none	1,120 cu. ft.	0.182	5
Roof pitch	5 in 12	10 in 12	0.212	20
Cumulative change due to architectural elements			0.212	41
Floor area	1,200 sq. ft.	2,600 sq. ft.		116*
Total change floor area and architectural			0.488	325

*An increase in floor area only.

Contrast this with a new home, well above the current national average of 2,500 square feet, on a similar lot in figure 5-15b. With higher ceilings and steep roof pitches (as much as twelve in twelve), not only have the homes grown to fill more of the lot, but building heights are much greater as well.[7] There is a strong reaction by many in the neighborhood that the new units are threatening the character of the area, which can be verified by BVR and SVR measurements.

In table 5-1, the details of incremental design changes are shown for a two-story house and the change in BVR. Having precise measurements of the character created by these changes provides better understanding of the problem and makes possible more opportunities to control it. The traditional tool for controlling building size was the floor area ratio. There are many things FAR does not address, however, such as ceiling height, the grand, two-story entrance hall, or roof pitches. The use of BVR provides the architect with design options other than losing a room. Will a prairie-style roofline provide the desired den? The architect may suggest trade-offs to the client. Landscaping presents additional opportunities; if mature trees are preserved, they can offset some increase in building volume.

Figures 5-11a and 5-11b compared two homes, the first retaining trees and the other built in the open. Lot area and home sizes are similar, as is the BVR; it is the LVR that shifts the SVR from negative to positive. In addition to the difference between the positive and negative site SVR, the woodland shelters the home, while on the cleared site the home is silhouetted against the sky, enhancing the impact of the BVR. It is far better to preserve trees, as shown in the above example, than to have to wait for twenty to fifty years for new landscaping to mature. Preservation of natural tree cover is beneficial for wildlife and is the best land cover to help water or air quality and global warming. The combination of volume measures allows for creative control of a development's character. The building and landscape volumes combined represent a way to look at the environment and manipulate both the building and vegetative masses. The volume measures also enable planners to quantify more precisely the results of a teardown, such as the McMansion. The BVR obviously addresses the differences in the two homes seen in figures 5-15a and 5-15b, as would the SVR.

D/H

The relationship of buildings to spaces is particularly important in urban design and helps to distinguish the three urban types— auto-urban, urban, and urban core. D/H is a measure of enclosure based on the distance across as space divided by the height of the enclosing buildings (see chapter 1). A D/H of one means the distance across the space is the same as the height of the surrounding buildings: for example, a street or space that measures sixty feet across surrounded by a five-story building. At values of less than one, the degree of enclosure is considered high. A person standing on one side of the sixty-foot space would have to look up at nearly a forty-five degree angle to see the roofline of the five-story building on the other side of the space.[8] To look up at rooflines involves a real intent. As D/H declines it takes more effort to look at the tops of buildings; the angle is about sixty degrees when the D/H declines to 0.5. A D/H of one to four is considered ideal for urban spaces such as squares or plazas. When spaces exceed a D/H of five, the degree of enclosure is weakened. This occurs even when the surrounding buildings occupy nearly 360 degrees around the space. Figures 5-16 through 5-19 illustrate D/H values of 0.25, 0.5, 1.0, and 2.0, respectively.

Figure 5-16. D/H = 0.25.

Figure 5-17. D/H = 0.5.

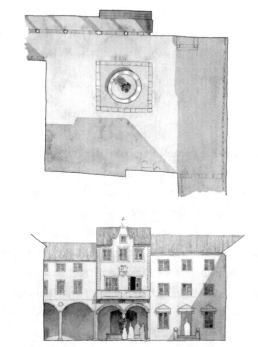

Figure 5-18. D/H = 1.0.

Figure 5-19. D/H = 2.0.

The D/H applies to streets and other public spaces. In general, streets will be more enclosing than a public space. Typically, public spaces—plazas, squares, parks, or other types of urban space—should have a D/H at least twice that of streets leading to them. This should be kept in mind when developing street standards and planning spaces. There are other pedestrian spaces that lead off the streets, such as pedestrian alleys or small, semipublic spaces, with lower D/H values and a more intimate feel. It is not uncommon to find a higher degree of enclosure in these pedestrian areas than in the street.

The D/H is an excellent measure of the differences between urban, urban core, and auto-urban. Urban core is best distinguished from the other two urban types by the inhuman scale of the buildings or D/H values. Most urban core streets will have D/H values of less than 0.3 and buildings over twenty stories, as seen in figure 5-20. An urban core street with an 80-foot right-of-way would only need 260-foot-high buildings (twenty stories) to provide a D/H of 0.3. Plazas may have D/H values closer to 1.0; for example, a space 300 feet wide surrounded by twenty-story buildings has a D/H of 1.15. The exception to this would be large public spaces such as Central Park in New York, the Boston Common, or Chicago's lakefront.

Auto-urban environments have a weak sense of enclosure, with D/H values often in excess of eight. The aerial view in figure 5-21 of an auto-urban corridor clearly shows the character type, with parking, roads, and landscaping spreading buildings apart. The standard, L-shaped shopping center does not really provide enclosure, even where there is no break between buildings. Figure 5-22 looks at one of two buildings in an L-shaped shopping center, where from the viewer's position at one of the out-lot buildings that are the third side of the parking area, the D/H is about eight and the building height (twenty-two to thirty feet) is not sufficient to create a feeling of enclosure. The automobile destroys the sense of a pedestrian space by dominating the foreground and requiring the pedestrian to be on the alert for moving vehicles. In addition, the many freestanding buildings found in auto-urban strip commercial areas means that horizontal enclosure will be incomplete, with buildings around a space occupying between 180 and 270 degrees.

Until the last century, most urban spaces were pedestrian precincts. The automobile has wreaked havoc with the quality

Figure 5-20. Urban core enclosure and scale. Chicago, Illinois.

Figure 5-21. Auto-urban: lack of enclosure and parking lot domination. Palm Beach County, Florida.

Figure 5-22. Cars in foreground, diminished buildings in background. West Jordan, Utah.

Figure 5-23. Cars along street allow enclosure. Annapolis, Maryland.

Figure 5-24. Lack of horizontal enclosure in suburban. Lake Villa, Illinois.

of space defined by D/H, as shown in figure 5-22. The pedestrian must walk through a sea of automobiles to reach the buildings. This is a far less pleasant environment even than a sidewalk lined with cars on one side (figure 5-23). The problem is that when parking and streets take up far more than half the land, there is no escape. The only question is where one experiences the auto-urban environment. The concept of pulling buildings to the street line and using on-street parking to create an urban space along the street fails. The reason for this failure is that the large parking lot does not disappear, but simply moves to the rear so that most customers cannot find a parking space on the street and are condemned to walk to the urban street through a lot. The development will have very high D/H values regardless of where parking is located.

While D/H can be used as a measure of sub-urban or rural environments, it is not particularly useful as a means of distinguishing among these types. The problem with the sub-urban type is that the horizontal enclosure is lost (see figure 5-24), so that one sees through to spaces in the rear; thus, even if D/H is measured across a street, the result does not account for the additional views to borrowed space. Further, vegetative masses are not accounted for by D/H. It is not recommended that D/H be applied to sub-urban character types. But D/H confirms the concern raised by the too-big house or teardown phenomena—that these buildings alter the character of the area. Older neighborhoods of ranch, bungalow, or Cape Cod housing types are quite low (sixteen to twenty-four feet in height). The modern, two-story home with a height of thirty-two to forty feet will increase the sense of enclosure, particularly when the units are built to the setback lines, which often results in mature trees being lost.

D/H becomes useful not in defining rural areas, because the number would be so large, but in defining types of rural spaces defined by woodlands and tree lines. Tree-lined or wooded areas can define spaces. They are most often found in rural character types and range from highly enclosed, somewhat akin to urban spaces, to those that have a bare sense of enclosure, even when they surround an area (see chapter 1 and the rural design chapter of the second book, *A Guide to Planning for Community Character*).

Scale

Both D/H and BVR provide information on scale. There are several more scale measures that are also useful in describing community character, including human, contextual, and social.

Measuring human scale is important because it addresses the relationship of humans to the built environment. In homes, walking from a room with a normal, eight-foot ceiling into a space with a cathedral ceiling presents a different spatial experience. The difference in a two-story house and a twenty-story condominium is also easily perceived. How do we measure more subtle differences of scale? Building volumes quickly reach numbers that are too large to be useful. For example, a relatively common three-story urban building, forty feet wide and eighty feet deep, has 134,400 cubic feet. A ten-story building with twenty thousand square feet of floor space has 2,600,000 cubic feet. The Japanese use the size of a tatami mat and specify room sizes in the number of mats. The tatami is about three feet by six feet and so approximates a prone human, and thus is an indicator of human scale. We can use the human figure in a similar manner. The human-scale unit is a volume six feet on a side, or thirty-six square feet and ten feet high (360 cubic feet; see chapter 1, figure 1-17). The height of ten feet makes it comparable to the site volume ratio, where the volume is divided by ten feet, and floor area ratio, which does not address height. The sidewalls of the human-scale unit are sixty square feet in area.

It is important to understand social scale when measuring human scale. Social scale relates human scale to actual human activities and social interactions that would occur in spaces. Edward T. Hall classified different human activities as intimate, personal, social, and public.[9] The scale of these spaces is based on the interaction of people in these situations. Hall broke each of these into a near and far phase, and there is another scale event that is related to special types of spaces. While the science is far from precise, it is possible to set ranges to the size of exterior spaces that meet these different criteria. Table 5.2 presents a scale for evaluating exterior spaces.

The intimate-scale space is very small, and humans in it would be in very close contact. Intense privacy by an individual may be desired. Two people standing in the space can easily

Table 5-2. Spatial scale types and measurements

Classification	Human scale	Square feet	Minimum width of space (ft.)	Acres
Intimate	1–4	36–144	4–7	0.00016–0.00033
Informal	6–20	216–720	8–13	0.005–0.016
Formal	40–400	19–60	60–120	0.03–0.33
Event	1,000–20,000	7,200–720,000	134–424	1.65–16.53

whisper or talk. The informal space is the size of a small private garden. People within the space can generally discern facial expressions and talk without having to project their voices. At the formal scale, one reaches the size of a suburban lot (about one-third of an acre), which is the farthest distance at which one could recognize a face. Event scales are much larger, with a football, baseball, or soccer stadium fitting within this space. Here people surrounding the field can discern the action, but cannot recognize one another on the opposite side of the facility. Designers of spaces need to keep in mind the social scale so that the space and the proposed activity are compatible. A small restaurant can function well at the informal scale but will be lost at the event scale, unless the space is broken into smaller units—in which case one risks losing a sense of the larger space, experiencing instead only a series of rooms.

Buildings also have scale problems when they become too large, as is the case with big-box uses or very tall buildings. Both lose their human scale. When the length of a building reaches the size of an event-scale use, the facade can become too massive; this is a problem for big-box uses, which can have over one hundred thousand square feet of floor area when the building is nothing but a box with few features. Tall buildings lose their human scale around twenty stories. Not only do the buildings dwarf humans, but they and their tops become difficult to view, requiring the viewer to work to take in the structure. When buildings or spaces become inhuman in scale, this requires the designer to break them up into human-scale components at ground or pedestrian level.

Maintaining the human scale for users is primarily an issue of relating and keeping one's interest. Once inside a large building, the space is broken into familiar units by shops or small-scale pedestrian areas. Malls, for example, have very large pedestrian spaces. Designers break them into three or four arms, often with angles, so that one can never see more than a portion of the space. These are further broken into smaller spaces by seating, plantings, and kiosks. In exterior architecture the concept of multiple levels of detailing—with a base, body, and top or cap treated as separate design elements—is understood, if not always used. In a small room we can appreciate very fine details that in a large room are lost until we get very close. What we see is heavily influenced by our distance from the building.[10] On a sidewalk, looking into store windows we can appreciate the rich, small-scale detailing on the frame of the window, which Louis Sullivan and other architects carried over to the early skyscrapers—buildings that were otherwise of an inhuman scale. That detail cannot be seen from across the street, where the window frame reads as a band with texture. The early designers of skyscrapers provided detail for the window shopper and believed that the building needed a base of only a story or two in height.[11] The skyscraper then had a middle and cap, which created a clear top element and often an interesting skyline. It is the base that is of critical interest, because this is what is seen from the street in spaces where humans interact. The top or skyline is usually viewed from distances, and with few exceptions we cannot experience it close-up.

The base of a skyscraper is rarely more than four human-scale units (forty feet in height). Not only does this area need windows to display items and interest the pedestrian, but the detailing of the solid building material can also provide engagement. The planting of street trees discourages one from looking up to the tops of the building and creates a more human space at ground level. It is by this attention to design that quality urban core environments can be created, despite the inhuman scale of the buildings.

Contextual scale refers to the relative scale between two buildings, two spaces, or building and vegetative masses. Contextual scale has a role to play in community character, particularly in micro-scale interactions within a neighborhood, and is useful in reviewing the compatibility of buildings to each other or their neighbors. People often perceive a building that is out of scale with its neighbor as being a threat to the character of the neighborhood. This can be measured with D/H, BVR, SVR, or human-scale units. The interface of residential with commercial, office, or industrial areas almost always results in a large

Figure 5-25. Building volume shows scale difference. Houston, Texas.

differential in scale. A change in scale is often a concern of residents at zoning hearings. They feel community character is threatened. It is the dramatic shift in scale that is destructive. The major exceptions to this are buildings the community perceives as important. The classic examples are churches, town halls, and county courthouses, which are often much larger than the surrounding commercial or residential structures in urban areas.[12] Placing a mid-rise building in a single-family neighborhood is clearly destructive of the area's character. Figure 5-25 shows a structure that is totally out of scale with the neighborhood, altering its character by the introduction of an urban core building mass in a suburban area.

An example of the application of the scale measure was prepared for Provincetown, Massachusetts, a nineteenth-century Cape Cod fishing village turned to tourism. The area's architectural heritage is very rich, with nearly half the town in one of several historic districts. The traditional zoning and building pattern resulted in several structures on each lot and a very fine-grained scale, with very small structures in most of the town. Even the sea captains' homes, the largest in the historic area, were not much larger, generally substantially less than four thousand square feet. The advent of condominiums for wealthy summer people, however, has resulted in the development of buildings that are totally out of keeping with the traditional scale of the community. Compare a traditional cottage-scale neighborhood (figure 5-26a) with a more recent townhouse complex in Provincetown (figure 5-26b). Another

Figure 5-26a. Small, human-scale building. Provincetown, Massachusetts.

Figure 5-26b. Townhouses out of scale. Provincetown, Massachusetts.

Figure 5-27a. Modest-scale building. Provincetown, Massachusetts.

Figure 5-27b. Large scale and shape out of character. Provincetown, Massachusetts.

area of Provincetown (figure 5-27a) shows a traditional neighborhood; a second set of townhouses (figure 5-27b) uses the traditional materials, but shape and scale do not fit. At the time they were built, these structures were derisively characterized by residents as the "Victorian outhouse" (5-26b) and the "Egyptian lighthouse" (5-27b). The residents correctly recognized that the scale was not compatible with Provincetown and did not fit the existing character.

Development can also threaten human scale when new buildings contrast with more modest residential or where the contrast is between new buildings and an historic urban scale. The Houston and Provincetown examples represent the residential contrasts. In many cities the older urban areas consist of blocks containing many small-scale buildings, with each read as an individual building though they are attached, forming a single building block (see figure 5-28a). The new building is about the same total area as the older block face, but the building reads as a single mass and is seen as out of scale (see figure 5-28b) with the historic area's character.

The contextual scale may be very large, as is often the case when office or large-scale commercial developments adjoin single-family areas, or it may be more subtle. It does not take much for a teardown to be out of scale, nor a more intense residential use. When scale is out of context, it disturbs the character of the area. The various measurement tools, whether applied to the total volume or the street facade, help to identify this problem.

Figure 5-28a. Fine-grained buildings with large overall mass. Annapolis, Maryland.

Figure 5-28b. Course-grained size increases apparent mass. Annapolis, Maryland.

In some communities, building scales may vary from block to block or even within a block. In that case the community must structure a means of analysis that defines an area to assure that future development is of an appropriate scale.

Community character and design are too complex to be copied from a template or to rely on a single measurement tool. Rather, there are many tools that can be used to identify major principles of design and to fit the needs of a particular area. In many cases, several measures should be combined to assist in making a determination. This is easiest for new construction, where it is possible to set standards for each character type and prohibit development that would fall in between two types. The planner will often find existing areas that are transitional, with elements of two or more types mixed together. The measurement ultimately may force one to acknowledge that the area is transitional and place it in the most appropriate category.

The measurements help to explain why an area is transitional. They also assist in explaining why a proposed use is different and alters the character of an area. These are valuable planning tools for identifying both possible threats to community character as well as opportunities for enhancing it.

CHAPTER 6 | *Conclusion*

While community character system began as a way to better address design, it has become a system for planning. A key element of the system is the relationship of scales and types of character to economic, social, environmental, or lifestyle conditions. They are based on the way people or markets interact with the character elements. These are real connections that cannot be ignored or wished away. They are capable of changing over time, as society and technology alter behavior. This is very important because it merges design with social and economic planning.

The land use plans found in most municipal comprehensive plans do not have this connection. Land use and density are just categories or numbers in a land use chapter of a plan that contains a map of the proposed future. Unfortunately this is not systematically linked to good design, nor is it linked to social, economic, environmental, or lifestyle elements. Too often, communities make planning or zoning decisions without understanding that these choices will affect the quality of life in the community. The community character system links character and land use decisions to these impacts so that officials and the public can evaluate them. Community character is superior to the current reliance on density and land use, and should replace them as the basis for community planning.

It is important for the type of character to be discussed and debated as part of developing a municipal plan, because its linkages help to envision what the community will be like if the plan is followed. The social and economic impacts of these decisions should further inform the debate. While shifting the balance among types is valid, it should be recognized that all the character types meet the needs of some segment of the population, and that group will resist change unless the alternative type can also meet their desires. Elected officials have difficulty understanding citizen concerns about the character of their neighborhood, other than as a window into the opinions of voters. The community character system provides a vocabulary and method of measurement that facilitates the discussion of character goals for a community. The social, economic, and environmental links promote a far broader discussion of the plan for the community's character. It is not uncommon for different sections of plans to have conflicts between goals in different chapters of the plan; for example, land use goals can create problems for transportation planning, or a desired economic or tax ratable goal may conflict with lifestyle or character goals. Community character promotes a better understanding of the relationship of these elements so that planners and citizens can have a dialogue about the pros and cons of any particular proposal.

Some elements of the system are more important as descriptors, such as regional types, to understand the nature of a community and its larger context. The notion of metropolitan form and the problems of protecting the freestanding character of a community are important issues in planning, yet they have received little attention over the past forty years. The mere recognition of these issues is important, and if that results in more effective regional planning it would be a substantial benefit. The mega form has great potential for urban cores and transit-oriented development.

Without a common vocabulary and measurement system, the discussion of character is subjective, and comments that a particular use will change character are written off as NIMBY rhetoric. But applying the community character analysis to a proposed development or zoning map amendment enables the question of whether there will be a change in character to be objectively measured. The system displays the true future character and whether the proposal is consistent with the adopted municipal plan. Measurement using the community character triangle provides the tool to test alternatives until the community understands and supports the proposed future.

Community character is a very flexible system consisting of principles and measurements; it is not a template to be copied. Applying these principles and measurements provides the ability to be flexible. For example, the urban street needs enclosure (the principle), and D/H (the measurement) allows one to evaluate the combination of street right-of-way, setback, and building height to ensure that the desired character is provided. This permits many combinations to be used, all of which provide the needed enclosure without mandating a specific template be universally adopted. The analysis allows municipal or developer flexibility.

In this volume, the intent was to describe the principles and relationships that create specific character types. The second book, *A Guide to Planning for Community Character*, provides a guide to using the system for different character classes and types, and for developing a comprehensive plan using the community character system. The link of character types and scale to transportation is also explored, as well as planning for the future using community character to address sustainability and energy. This current volume presents the description and principles of the different aspects of community character and the types of measures that may used to evaluate a development or area. The second book contains chapters that explore the critical elements of designing each of three major character classes and their types. It is far more design-oriented, but is not a template either. It focuses on the distinctions between the types and on dealing with environmental issues, while also seeking to integrate all the different aspects of community character that are dealt with separately in this book.

Each of the three character classes has distinct design requirements. These will be covered in greater detail, along with the elements that distinguish types within a class. The challenges of modern urban design will also be explored. We have a major problem in that, without structured parking it is impossible to create an urban environment that has true urban enclosure. The three chapters on urban, sub-urban, and rural design provide a comprehensive design approach for all character types. The discussion focuses on tools such as zoning standards and applying the principles, rather than providing a single template to be followed by all.

In addition to a chapter on the comprehensive plan, another chapter will look at design. This is done from two perspectives. The first concerns how character type, scale, state, and form interact. The second holds that community character only addresses part of how design relates to character; the quality of a community design is also important. Ultimately, quality of a character type is a question of the skill of the designer in applying the micro-design elements, not the major character elements. It is possible to fully meet all the design requirements of a specific community character, and to do it well or poorly. Pure design then takes over, and this chapter addresses the design elements that need to be considered for quality.

A last chapter addresses the future. Most of the character types (except for two of the urban ones) have been present since soon after humans lived in fixed settlements. One can expect that all the types will continue to be used in the future. A pie chart for any period of history would have a very different distribution of the percentage of the population living in the different character types or different-scale communities compared to the present day. For most of history hamlets and villages would dominate the scale pie chart. Urban would be the dominant type because even rural hamlets and villages were urban communities with strongly enclosed streets and spaces. In the United States, rural took on a pattern of individual farms. The Industrial Revolution began a movement to towns and cities and the development of metropolitan areas. The late nineteenth century began the popularization of the suburbs, and they eventually became the place of residence of a major portion of the population, even in many towns and cities. The forces that have brought us to the current mix are dynamic and many are changing. The environmental crisis of global warming and energy consumption suggests that a different mix is needed, and technology may play a critical role in determining whether the automobile will continue to have a major shaping influence. The author's projections as to the future direction are contained in this last segment. These changes require significant changes in the way communities are planned and zoned. There needs to be more urban core and urban, and significantly reduced areas of auto-urban. Suburban and estate areas should also be reduced, but more importantly, their densities need to be increased. Lastly, regional planning must become viable and effective.

This book has presented community character in all its various components. Planners, planning commissions, elected officials, developers, and citizens interested in preserving, protecting, or planning their communities should be able to apply the principals and measurements presented here to their neighborhood, municipality, or development. The diversity of measurements should enable users to better understand the character of their community and its critical components. For those most concerned with the planning of the future it offers a new planning tool. For those most concerned with protecting their neighborhood it provides ways to determine if the character will be changed and to present the findings in an objective fashion. It eliminates the subjectivity that has previously made discussing community character difficult. A shift in character can be defined with precision; often several of the measurements can be applied. Lastly, this volume presents a complete methodology to replace density and land use with a system that actually relates to design and character of communities, which should make it possible to develop better municipal plans.

Notes

INTRODUCTION

1. *Board of County Commissioners Teton County, Wyoming v. Crow*, 65 P.3d 720 (Wyo. 2003).

2. Seymour Toll, *Zoned American* (New York: Grossman Publishers, 1969), 151.

3. Andres Duany, Sandy Sorlien, and William Wright, *SmartCode and Manual* (Miami: New Urban Publications, 2005), C8. The Transect is supposed to replicate the transect as used in ecology, a representation of what is found along a cross-section line.

CHAPTER 1

1. Yoshinobu Ashihara, *Exterior Design in Architecture* (New York: Van Nostrand Reinhold, 1970), 21.

2. In planning rural landscapes, it is possible to have positive spaces that are enclosed by trees or landforms. This is a very specialized aspect of design.

3. Ashihara, *Exterior Design in Architecture*, 30. Ashihara uses examples of negative space as being natural. It is not truly natural, however, nor does it imply isolation in a larger landscape, but rather a focus on the surrounded building.

4. Edmund N. Bacon, *Design of Cities* (New York: Viking Press, 1967), 24.

5. Edward T. Hall, *The Hidden Dimension* (Garden City, N.Y.: Doubleday, 1966), 114.

6. Thomas Thiis-Evensen, *Archetypes of Urbanism*, trans. Scott Campbell (Oslo: Universitetsforlaget, 1999), 49.

7. Ibid., 48.

8. It is worth noting that the texture of certain materials can be bad or unsafe in particular applications, as with a slippery surface where there are lots of pedestrians.

9. Christopher Alexander, Sarah Ishikawa, and Murray Silverstein, *A Pattern Language* (New York: Oxford University Press, 1977), 558–60.

10. Kevin Lynch, *The Image of the City* (Cambridge, Mass.: MIT Press, 1960), 51.

11. Alexander, Ishikawa, and Silverstein, *Pattern Language*, 54.

12. In *Pattern Language*, Alexander, Ishikawa, and Silverstein identify a number of entrances as patterns: main gateways (pattern #53), a family of entrances (#102), main entrances (#110), entrance transitions (#112), and entrance rooms (#130).

13. The terms "hill" and "mountain" are often applied locally to name local features and are therefore not useful. The distinctions here relate to the national level, where mountains rise thousands of feet.

14. Tree lines (assumed here to be fifty to eighty feet tall) that are near the limit of the natural horizon two or more miles away will seem like the natural horizon itself as they have D/H values well over two hundred.

15. In general, land cover, forest, prairie, and wetlands are not considered a land use. Agriculture, open space or park, and vacant are generally as detailed as land use gets.

16. These included the Standard Industrial Classification System, managed by the U.S. Department of Labor, which was supplanted in 1997 by the North American Industrial Classification System.

17. Lane Kendig, *Performance Zoning* (Washington, D.C.: Planners Press, American Planning Association, 1980), 20.

18. In some cases, rural land is surveyed as running to the centerline of existing roads. The gross land area would exclude any land in the site dedicated to existing roads.

19. Lane Kendig, *New Standards for Nonresidential Uses*, Planning Advisory Series 405 (Chicago: American Planning Association, 1987). The concept dates back to zoning ordinances done in 1983 by Mr. Kendig.

20. Ibid., 8–11; and Kendig, *Too Big, Boring, and Ugly*, Planning Advisory Service 548 (Chicago: American Planning Association, 2004), 51–52.

21. A floor area ratio of one indicates a floor equal in area to the site. The division by ten means a building ten feet high covering the entire site would have a BVR of one.

CHAPTER 2

1. The term "settlement" will be used in the context of freestanding communities to mean the built-up or urbanized portion of the community, as opposed to its sphere of economic or social influence.

2. Avi Friedman, *Planning the New Suburbia* (Vancouver: UBC Press, 2002), 25.

3. Arthur B. Gallion and Simon Eisner, *The Urban Pattern* (New York: Van Nostrand, 1950), 278.

4. Joel Garreau, *Edge Cities* (New York: Doubleday, 1991), 5.

5. This was not the case for most of history, where communities grew house by house, with few exceptions. Most of these communities were group forms (chapter 4), where blocks came about because of natural evolution rather than structured growth.

6. To achieve this figure, a walking pace of three miles per hour, or 264 feet per minute, is applied to the diameter.

7. Cynthia L Girling and Kenneth I. Helphand, *Yard, Street, Park* (New York: J. Wiley, 1994), 135.

8. Anton C. Nelessen, *Visions for a New American Dream* (Chicago: APA Planners Press, 1994), 156.

9. Frank Jackson, *Sir Raymond Unwin* (London: A. Zwemmer, 1985), 147.

10. Spiro Kostof, *The City Shaped* (Boston: Little, Brown, 1991), 36.

11. This actually happened in Madison and Dane County, Wisconsin. The City of Madison dominated the county decision making and wanted an urban area, so it prohibited estate development in most of the county. This simply forced the market for this lifestyle into the next county and actually created longer work trips, thereby worsening sprawl.

12. Garreau, *Edge Cities*, 4.

13. Architectural Record, *Time-Saver Standards* (New York: F. W. Dodge, 1954), 345.

CHAPTER 3

1. Few of these people documented their application, but the rules were consciously or unconsciously used in the creation of important spaces.

2. Lewis Mumford, *The City in History* (New York: Harcourt, Brace, and World, 1961), 486.

3. Different physiographic environments—desert, short-grass prairie, Pacific forest, pine forests, and oak-hickory deciduous forests—are visual interpretations of some of these.

4. This is not always the case. Many areas in the Great Plains do not have good water, and rural water companies provide service. Rocky soils and high water tables should limit on-site systems, but individual states have not always been responsible in setting standards.

5. The natural congestion reflects activity levels, with the most intense areas needing congestion to bring all the uses together. Low congestion means there is a low volume of trips on a per-acre basis. This ignores actual road spacing, highway usage by commuters, or regional traffic.

6. There are downwind effects that pollute air even hundreds of miles away, and thus rural air quality can be badly damaged by distant urban areas.

7. The fact is that too often engineering has attempted to overcome nature. Cities are built in floodplains, and ultimately floods damage these metropolitan areas. Venice is not the only city sinking on unstable soil—it is just the most well-known and spectacular. For example, Mexico City and New Orleans, built on swamps, continue to sink as well.

8. A great many communities had streets that were passable only by pedestrian or pack animal and were not negotiable by carts or wagons.

9. In work over the last two decades, I have found that the presence or absence of trees in two otherwise-similar environments results in a higher rating for the image with the trees than the one without.

10. The problem of mandating ground floor commercial and then not having a market that supports this has developed in Annapolis, Chicago, and Boulder. A great many uses that occupy freestanding buildings have community or larger markets and are too large for many mixed-use environments.

11. Farmers who came to the market square with carts came early before the shoppers, unhitched and removed the draft animals from the carts and wagons, and used the vehicles as stalls for product display. In that way, the pedestrian mode ruled through the market time.

12. Major cities in the East and Midwest all had commercial strips along major roads that also generally had a streetcar route. In many cases these strips ran for miles. This form was mindlessly extended into the suburbs.

13. Quoted in Mumford, *City in History*, 485.

14. Randall Arendt, *Rural by Design* (Chicago: Planners Press, American Planning Association, 1994), 315–60.

15. Anton C. Nelessen, *Visions for a New American Dream* (Chicago: APA Planners Press, 1994), 88.

16. Not in my backyard (NIMBY) and citizens against virtually everything (CAVE).

17. The key exception to this is communities with performance zoning, where there is a mandatory open space requirement for clustered development, bonus increase in density compared to the cookie-cutter subdivision.

18. Frederick C. Pearson and others, *Land Use and Arterial Spacing in Suburban Areas* (Washington, D.C.: U.S. Department of Transportation, Federal Highway Administration, Urban Planning Division, 1977).

19. A shopping center generates nearly 43 trips per 1,000 square feet of leasable area. At 25,000 square feet of commercial per acre, that is 1,075 trips.

20. It is a general rule of thumb that the improved lot is 25 percent of the cost of the home. Thus, a $10,000 increase in the cost of a lot will result in a $40,000 increase in the cost of the home.

21. An open space ratio of zero is attainable today only where storm-water-detention facilities are permitted on individual lots. We recommend that detention always be on common open space so that it can be owned and maintained by the homeowners association, which generally means 5 to 15 percent open space.

22. Randall Arendt, *Growing Greener* (Washington, D.C.: Island Press, 1999), 5.

23. The land-treatment system is vastly preferable to package plants because they do not have upsets (where the plant discharges untreated sewerage) and do not discharge to streams.

24. Long Grove, Illinois, is a village with an estate-to-countryside character that encourages private streets and low government services. The village has no village real estate taxes, which is a policy in the comprehensive plan. Residents still pay taxes, however, to the school district and the county government.

25. This is based on forty-acre homesteads. In fact, the size of farms today would put them even further apart.

26. McHenry County, Illinois, in the Chicago metropolitan area, adopted agricultural zoning of 160 acres per house, sufficient to make residential development totally infeasible. The Illinois courts upheld the county's action when challenged. Some states even require very low-density agricultural zoning.

CHAPTER 4

1. Spiro Kostof, *The City Shaped* (Boston: Little, Brown: 1991), 47–48.

2. Fumihiko Maki and Masato Ohtaka, "Some Thoughts on Collective Form," in *Structure in Art and in Science*, ed. Gyorgy Kepes (New York: G. Braziller, 1965), 117.

3. Ibid., 118.

4. A section of a mile square contains 640 acres. Quartering it results in a 160-acre quarter section. Quartering it again results in the 40-acre parcel often used to homestead a farm.

5. City of Franklin, Comprehensive Master Plan, August 1992 (Lane Kendig Inc., now Kendig Keast Collaborative). This plan detail was the result of planners working with the city engineer, who had regional experience and wanted road and utilities planned to a level where new lines would not need be retroactively installed.

6. Ebenezer Howard, *Garden Cities of To-Morrow* (1902; repr., Cambridge, Mass.: MIT Press, 2007).

7. See Gallion and Eisner, *Urban Pattern*, 279.

8. Christopher Scarre, ed., *Past Worlds: The Times Atlas of Archaeology* (New York: Times Books, 1988), 85. The remains of Paleolithic camps and the earliest hamlets and villages all show this pattern. A simple building pattern is repeated at random, leaving spaces in between for activities.

9. Maki and Ohtaka, "Some Thoughts on Collective Form," 120.

10. Kostof, *The City Shaped*, 43.

11. Bernard Rudofsky, *Architecture Without Architects* (Garden City, N.Y.: Doubleday, 1964).

12. Edward Allen, *Stone Shelters* (Cambridge, Mass.: MIT Press, 1969), 80–81.

13. Leonardo Benevolo, *The History of the City* (Cambridge, Mass.: MIT Press, 1980), 7–26.

14. Duany, Sorlien, and Wright, *SmartCode and Manual*.

15. Mass grading is where the entire site is regraded to create a space that is engineered for sewer (storm water and sanitary) and roads, rather than working with existing topography.

16. Paolo Soleri, *Arcology: The City in the Image of Man* (Cambridge, Mass.: MIT Press, 1969), 13. Soleri uses the term "arcology" to define what is called here "mega structures."

17. Gurnee Mills, a super-regional, off-price mall in Gurnee, Illinois, has seen new anchors added, major anchors change and be enlarged, and an ice-skating rink added as a use instead of a retail store. Regional malls in the Chicago area have increased floor area by converting at-grade parking to parking structures.

18. Soleri's *Arcology* presents thirty separate mega structure plans, pp. 36–122.

19. Paul D. Spreiregen, *Urban Design: The Architecture of Towns and Cities* (New York: McGraw-Hill, 1965), 33.

20. Howard, *Garden Cities of To-Morrow*.

21. Jackson, *Sir Raymond Unwin*, 147.

22. Spreiregen, *Urban Design*, 32.

23. Jackson, *Sir Raymond Unwin*, 147–48.

CHAPTER 5

1. In central Illinois, distances are four to sixteen miles. In Wyoming this increases to over forty, with the average being closer to ten. In the East, distances tend to be lower. In all environments, distances are closer along early roads, where traffic was heavy and travel was by horse.

2. Triangular diagrams are commonly used to class soils by three basic types: sand, silt, or clay.

3. This is true because counties typically have build-out periods that are far in excess of fifty years, so the total population provided by even low-density zoning is huge. For cities this may not be the case, however, because they typically grow by annexation and thus have more limited undeveloped land area.

4. SAVES is planning software developed by Kendig Keast Collaborative that enables the evaluation of proposed plan alternatives or zoning amendments. CommunityViz, developed by Placeways LLC, is planning software that can project or analyze future development and is linked to maps.

5. FEMA floodplain regulations permit filling the floodplain, and in too many parts of the country wetlands are still filled. Therefore federal protection is not all it may seem to the casual observer.

6. The first number indicates the rise in inches of the roof compared to inches of run. A twelve in twelve pitch is a forty-five degree angle.

7. The 1950s ranch house would be fifteen to sixteen feet high, and a two-story between twenty-four and twenty-five feet high. The modern home on a similar lot would be thirty-two to thirty-four feet high, a large visual difference.

8. Paul D. Spreiregen, *Urban Design: The Architecture of Towns and Cities* (New York: McGraw-Hill, 1965), 71. Human vision looking straight ahead has about a thirty-degree view above the horizontal. Thus one needs to look up to see the skyline.

9. Hall, *Hidden Dimension*.

10. Ashihara, *Exterior Design in Architecture*, 52–55. This text provides an excellent discussion and photos showing the change in building texture and elements with the viewer's distance.

11. The first floor of many commercial buildings is often equal to two stories, between twenty and twenty-six feet in height.

12. Note that this is changing. Milwaukee is a city of neighborhood churches and taverns. These uses were neighborhood uses, where the local area has a strong identity. As modern churches shift from neighborhood to community or subregional uses, their importance to the neighborhood declines; therefore, major scale differences, instead of strengthening the neighborhood's identity, are considered a threat because the flow of cars driven by outsiders changes it from a local source of pride to a nuisance.

Index

Figures/photos/illustrations are indicated by a "f"
and tables by a "t."

Aalto, Alvar, 126
agriculture
    community character word usage and, 34–35
    cropland, 108f
    grazing land, 108f
    land and un-zoned, scattered residential, 42f
    rural class and, 108–109
    zoning, 176n26
air quality, 75, 175n6
Alberti, Leon Battista, 91
Alexander, Christopher, 117
architectural space, 10, 10f
architectural style, 18–19
Architecture Without Architects (Rudofsky), 119
arcology, 176n16, 177n18
Arcosanti, 124, 126f. *See also* Soleri, Paolo
Arendt, Randall, 93, 100
articulated space, 27
artificial horizon, 14, 14f, 93f
Ashihara, Yoshinobu, 173n3, 177n10
asymmetry, 20–21, 21f. *See also* symmetry
auto-urban, 35, 82f, 87–91, 89f, 175n12
axial space, 19, 19f

Bacon, Edmund, 13
the blob/sheet (status quo), 136–137
blocks, 48–49, 49f. *See also* composite communities
borrowed horizon, 13–14, 14f
borrowed space, 12, 12f
    in cluster development, 96f
    clustering to create, 98f
    park providing open, 96f

undeveloped land and open, 95f
    boundaries, 43–44, 45
building coverage, 29, 29f
building volume ratio (BVR), 32, 32f. *See also* volume
    ratios
BVR. *See* building volume ratio

canopy, 14, 14f
carbon footprint, 76
castles, 125f. *See also* mega forms
CAVE people (citizens against virtually everything),
    95
CBD. *See* central business district
ceiling, 13
central business district (CBD), 54, 56, 58, 60–64. *See
    also* shopping district
chaos, 17, 17f
child play, 79
cities
    fortified edge, 41f
    large sectors or, 57–58
    small districts and, 56–57
citizens against virtually everything. *See* CAVE
    people
Citta Nuova, 127
city center, 56f, 58f
City Planning According to Artistic Principles (Sitte),
    31
The City in History (Mumford), 68
Ciudad Lineal, 134
cliff dwelling, 125f
clusters, 48–49, 49f, 92f, 108. *See also* composite
    communities
color, 18
commercial, 126f

communities/municipalities
    community character word usage, 34
    composite area with multiple, 44f
    towns and, 54–55
community character
    challenges for future and, 7–8
    density and one dwelling unit per acre, 4f
    density and three dwelling units per acre, 4f
    estate commercial, 5f
    high-quality urban and design, 6f
    introduction, 1–8
    as planning system, 167–168
    poor design and low-quality urban, 6f
    six reasons for understanding, 2–3
    type and area, 52t
    urban commercial, 5f
    why, 2–7
community character classes/types
    environmental aspects of, 73t
    physical, environmental, economic, social attributes and, 69–80
    physical attributes of, 70t
    rural class and, 102–109
    social and economic attributes of, 77t
    special character types and, 109–110
    sub-urban class and, 91–102
    urban class and, 80–91, 175n7
community character measurement, 139, 170–171
    aerial photo of Amarillo, Tx, 143f
    average home size and, 177nn6–7
    community character diagram and, 141–150
    community state and scale and, 140–141
    desired future character options, 149f
    D/H and, 157–160
    diagram, 142f
    existing community character map, 143f
    measuring community character and, 141–150
    plotting past community character, 145f
    possible future character options, suburban or urban, 146f
    rules for plotting existing land use and, 150–152
    scale and, 161–166
    using open space to define character, 147f
    volume ratios and, 152–157
    zoning and, 177n3
community character word usage
    community/municipality, 34

    designer's lexicon of, 33–35
    rural/countryside/agriculture/natural, 34–35
    sub-urban/suburban/suburb/suburbia/slurb, 34
    urban/auto-urban/urban core/urbanization, 35
community forms
    compositional, group and mega, 113f
    compositional forms and, 113–117
    conclusion, 137
    group form and, 117–123
    mega forms and, 123–129
    planning for, 129–130
    regional, metropolitan and, 130–137
    regional forms and, 111–137
    structural forms and, 112–113
community scale, 14, 46t
    common land uses and, 64t
    community state and, 45–60
    distance between communities and, 177n1
    hamlets, blocks, clusters and, 48–49
    large cities, sectors and, 57–58
    megalopoleis and, 59
    metropoleis and, 58–59
    neighborhood design and, 52–54
    regional planning and, 59–60
    small cities, districts and, 56–57
    towns, communities and, 54–55
    villages, neighborhoods and, 49–51
community state
    community scale and, 45–60
    composite communities and, 42–45
    conclusion, 66
    context and scale, 37–66
    distance between communities and, 177n1
    freestanding communities and, 40–42
    freestanding village surrounded by open land, 140f
    freestanding/composite scale and, 38f
    scale, economics and, 60–66
    view to center of Schwerte, Germany, 140f
    view to suburb separated by green space, 140f
CommunityViz, 147, 177n4
composite communities, 37
    boundaries, 44–45
    community state and, 42–45
    identity in, 43–44
    road and density dividing two neighborhoods and, 40f

compositional forms, 112
axial streets, 118f
blocks divided into lots, 114f
city of Franklin comprehensive master plan, 176n5
cluster plan, 117f
community forms and, 113–117
curvilinear road with natural feel, 117f
landscaped and long cul-de-sac, 116f
neighborhood plan, 115f
open space in cluster, 117f
parkway and drainage used to organize, 116f
schematic plan for garden city, 118f
squares used as organization, 116f
congestion, 72, 101, 105, 107, 175n5
continuity, 17. *See also* harmony
contrast
chaos and, 17, 17f
dominance and, 17, 18f
harmony and, 17, 17f
monotony and, 16–17, 17f
cookie-cutter zoning, 28, 175n17
Le Corbusier, 3
countryside
character, very large lot with home in woodland, 107f
community character word usage and, 34–35
development, 106f
fully developed site, 107f
lotting patterns shown not protecting character, 106f
rural class and, 105–107
crime/safety, 80, 99, 102
cul-de-sacs, 49, 116f, 121

da Vinci, Leonardo, 15
defined spaces, 26
density, 28
composite community, road and, 40f
dwelling units per acre, 29f
net, gross and net-net, 29
one dwelling unit per acre, 4f
three dwelling units per acre, 4f
descriptive terms
architectural space, 10, 10f
designer's lexicon of, 10–16
garden-like, 10
landscape, 10

mass, 11
planes, 12–14
scale, 14–16
space, 11–12
desert, 25
design
with group form, 119–123
high- and poor-quality, 6f
rules, 174n1
designer's lexicon, 9
community character word usages, 33–35
descriptive terms, 10–16
land use and zoning terms, 27–33
landscape terms, 22–27
organizational design terms, 19–22
qualitative terms, 16–19
D/H. *See* distance/height ratio
diagrams, 141–150, 142f, 177n2
distance/height ratio (D/H), 31f, 85, 88, 177n8
auto-urban, lack of enclosure and parking lot domination, 159f
cars along street allow enclosure, 160f
cars in foreground, diminished buildings in background, 160f
community character measurement and, 157–160
D/H = 0.5, 158f
D/H = 0.25, 158f
D/H = 1.0, 158f
D/H = 2.0, 158f
lack of horizontal enclosure in suburban, 160f
LSR and, 31
urban core enclosure and scale, 159f
districts, small cities and, 56–57
dominance, 17, 18f

economic attributes
child play, 79
economic role, 77
encounter level, 78
function, 76–77
opportunities for relaxation, 79–80
physical, environmental and social, 76–80
privacy, 79
safety from crime, 80
site of social contract, 78–79
workforce, 77–78

economic role, 77

economics, scale and, 60–66

edges

    car dealer against residential and land use, 44f

    fortified wall, gate tower and, 41f

    freestanding communities and, 40–42

    hilltop fortified city, 41forganizational design
        terms and, 21–22

    river, wall and, 22f

    sprawl prevented by hard, 40–41

    topography and fitted sharp, 41f

enclosed/enclosing space, 26

enclosure, 11, 31, 83f, 86f

encounter level, 78

entrances/gateways, 22

environmental attributes

    air quality, 75

    carbon footprint, 76

    heat island effect, 75–76

    impervious surface ratio, 73

    on-site resource protection, 73–74

    physical, economic and social, 72–76

    storm-water runoff, 74

    water quality per acre, 74

    water quality per person, 74–75

estate, 99–102

    commercial with wooded site, 101f

    formal residential, 100f

    informal residential, 100f

    office with eighty percent open space, 101f

    real estate taxes and, 176n24

    sprawl, 43f

Euclid v. Ambler Realty Co., 2

event scale, 16

Exterior Design in Architecture (Ashihara), 177n10

FAR. See floor area ratio

farmers, 175n11

farming communities, 48, 104

farmland

    acres/parcels of land for, 176n4

    distance between farms and, 176n25

    farming hamlets and, 49f

    land cover and, 25

    rural class and, 103f

FEMA floodplain regulations, 177n5

figure-ground (building coverage), 31, 31f

fire services, 71, 72, 82, 99, 102, 105

flat landforms, 23

floodplains, 45, 73, 136, 177n5

floor area ratio (FAR), 29–30, 30f, 174n21

floor/ground plane, 13

forest, 24, 174n15

forest edge, 26–27

formal scale, 15–16

freestanding communities, 37, 39f

    community state and, 40–42

    edges, 40–42

    separation, 42

    service area and spacing of, 40f

    "settlement" and, 174n1

function, social/economic attributes and, 76–77

garden-like, 10, 10f, 70, 91f, 95

gated communities, 44

gateways/entrances, 22

Geographic Information System maps, 31

global warming, 7, 55

green roof, 76

green space, 92

green volume, 93

greenbelt, 132, 132f

gross density, 29

ground plane/floor, 13

group forms, 112–113, 174n5

    commercial center fits topography, 124f

    community forms and, 117–123

    concept plan for new, 122f

    design with, 119–123

    half-timbered homes, 119f

    mixed uses on street face, 123f

    Paleolithic camps as, 176n8

    pedestrian street, 119f

    single-family urban, 124f

    street of stairs to account for topography,
        119f

    structure of, 117–119

    subdivision entrance, 122f

    suburban single-family, 125f

    townhouses to sidewalk, 124f

    varied setbacks, 123f

    on vaulted stone buildings, 118f

    walled yard at corner, 123f

    widened street for restaurant, 120f

A Guide to Planning for Community Character (Kendig), 7, 76, 103, 151, 169–170
Gurnee Mills mall, 176n17

Hall, Edward T., 161
hamlets, 48–49, 49f. *See also* freestanding communities
harmony, 17, 17f
Haussmann, Baron, 111, 112
heat island effect, 75–76
hedge, as wall, 12f
hierarchical space, 20, 20f
Holy Roman Empire, 54
horizon, 13f
    artificial, 14, 14f, 93f
    borrowed, 13–14, 14f
    landscape and view across field to, 10f
horizontal enclosure, 31
housing type, 71
Howard, Ebenezer, 116
human scale, 15, 15f

identity, in composite communities, 43–44
impervious surface ratio, 30, 30f, 73
independent regions, 38
Industrial Revolution, 82
infinite scale, 16
infinite space, 12, 12f, 16, 26
informal scale, 15
intensity
    building coverage and, 29, 29f
    density and, 28–29
    FAR and, 29–30
    impervious surface ratio and, 30, 30f
    lot size and, 28
    open space ratio and, 30, 30f
interior space, 27
intimate scale, 15

Japan
    architecture in, 15, 127
    scale in, 161

Kendig Keast Collaborative, 107, 177n4
Kikutake, Kiyonori, 127

land cover, 174n15
    desert, farmland, mixed and prairie, 25

forest, 24
    savannah, 24–25
land use, 71
    edge and car dealer against residential, 44f
    four general use categories and, 27
    zoning terms and, 27–33
landforms, 22
    flat and undulating, 23
    mountainous, 24, 173n13
    ridges and valleys, 24
    rolling, 23, 23f
    rugged, 24
landscape, view across field to horizon, 10f
landscape surface ratio (LSR), 30, 31, 31f
landscape terms
    designer's lexicon of, 22–27
    land cover, 24–25
    landforms, 22–24
    landscape types, 25–27
landscape types, 25
    articulated and interior spaces, 27
    defined, enclosed, infinite and enclosing spaces, 26
    forest edge, 26–27
    undifferentiated spaces, 26
landscape volume ratio (LVR), 32, 32f. *See also* volume ratios
large cities/sectors, 57–58
Lee Harris Pomeroy Architects, 126
library, 126f
linear, 132f, 133–134, 134f
lot size, 28, 175n20
LSR. *See* landscape surface ratio
LVR. *See* landscape volume ratio

Manitou Station plans, 128f
mass, 11
mass grading, 176n15
McMansions, 155, 157
mega forms, 112, 113, 176n16
    Arcosanti, 124, 126f
    cliff dwelling, 125f
    community and, 123–129
    design with, 128–129
    existing, 124–127
    Manitou Station plans, 128f
    precast, modular, 127f

Schloss Lichtenstein, 125f
    stairs to town hall level, 127f
    Taos Pueblo, 126f
    town hall, commercial and library, 126f
    Weyerhaeuser headquarters building, 127, 128f
megalopoleis, 59
metropoleis, 58–59
metropolitan forms
    blob or sheet, 136–137
    community, regional and, 130–137
    greenbelt, 132
    greenbelt, star, linear, satellite, organic, 132f
    linear, 133–134
    organic, 135–136
    satellite, 134–135
    star, 133
metropolitan regions, 38
mixed land cover, 25
monotony, 16–17, 17f
"monster" houses, 155, 157
Moshe Safdie and Associates, 126
mountainous landforms, 24, 173n13
Mumford, Lewis, 68, 91
municipalities/communities, 34, 44f

natural
    community character word usage and, 34–35
    forest character, 109f
    residential development retaining natural character and, 109f
    rural class and, 108–109
    wildlife inhabitants, 109f
negative space, 11–12, 11f, 173n3
neighborhood design, 52–54
neighborhoods, 49–51
Nelessen, Anton C., 52
net density, 29
net-net density, 29
New Urbanist movement/model, 3, 47, 94, 154
NIMBYs (not in my backyard), 95, 126, 168
nodes, 21, 21f

on-site resource protection, 73–74
open space ratio, 30, 30f, 175n21
organic, 132f, 135–136
organizational design terms
    axial space, 19, 19f

designer's lexicon of, 19–22
    edges, 21–22, 22f
    entrances or gateways, 22
    hierarchical space, 20, 20f
    nodes, 21, 21f
    pathways, 21, 21f
    sequential space, 19–20, 20f
    symmetry types, 20–21, 20f, 21f

Paleolithic camps, 176n8
parks, 53, 78, 115–116
pathways, 21, 21f
A Pattern Language (Alexander), 117, 173n12
pedestrians
    plaza, 85f
    precincts, 84f, 87, 96
    roads/walkways, 50, 119f
    space, 89f
Perry, Clarence, 117
physical attributes
    congestion, 72
    environmental, economic and social, 69–72
    housing type, 71
    land use, 71
    road spacing, 72
    service and utilities, 71–72
    spatial quality, 69–70
    spatial relationships, 70–71
    transit suitability, 72
Placeways LLC, 177n4
planes
    canopy, 14, 14f
    ceiling, 13
    floor or ground, 13
    horizon, 13–14, 13f, 14f
    roof, 14, 14f, 76
    screens, 12–13, 12f, 13f
    skyline, 13, 13f, 104f, 177n8
    walls, 12, 12f
plant units, 33, 33f, 34f
police services, 71, 82, 99, 102, 105
populations, 45
    how businesses relate to, 61
    large cities or sectors, 57
    megalopoleis, 59
    towns and communities, 54
positive space, 11, 11f, 31, 173n2

prairie, 25, 174n15

privacy, 79

qualitative terms
    architectural style, 18–19
    color, 18
    contrast, 16–17
    designer's lexicon of, 16–19
    rhythm, 17–18, 18f
    texture, 18, 18f

real estate taxes, 176n24

regional forms. *See also* metropolitan forms
    blob or sheet, 136–137
    community, metropolitan and, 130–137
    community forms and, 111–137

regional planning, 59–60

relative scale, 14–15, 15f

relaxation, opportunities for, 79–80

rhythm, 17–18, 18f

ridges, 24

road spacing, 72

roads/walkways, pedestrian, 50, 119f

rolling landforms, 23, 23f

roof, 14, 14f, 76

rugged landforms, 24

rules for plotting existing land use
    community character measurement and, 150–152
    rural, 150
    sub-urban, 150
    urban, 151–152

rural, 34–35

Rural by Design (Arendt), 93

rural class
    agriculture and natural, 108–109
    community character, classes and types and,
        102–109
    countryside and, 105–107
    distance between farms in, 176n25
    fortified town on hill and, 104f
    home on low ridge disturbs skyline and, 104f
    large farm buildings viewed as part of landscape
        and, 103f
    rural landscape and, 103f
    village in background and, 103f

rural regions, 38

rural/countryside/agriculture/natural, 34–35

safety from crime, 80, 99, 102

Sant'Elia, Antonio, 127

satellite, 132f, 134–135

savannah, 24–25

SAVES, 147, 177n4

scale
    building volume shows difference in, 164f
    community, 14, 45–60
    community character measurement and, 161–166
    community state, context and, 37–66
    course-grained size increases apparent mass, 166f
    economics and, 60–66
    event, 16
    fine-grained buildings with large overall mass,
        166f
    formal, 15–16
    freestanding/composite state and, 38f
    human, 15, 15f
    infinite, 16
    informal, 15
    intimate, 15
    in Japan, 161
    large scale and shape out of character, 165f
    modest-scale building, 165f
    relative, 14–15, 15f
    shifts in, 177n12
    skyscrapers and, 177n11
    small, human-scale building, 164f
    social, 15–16
    spatial scale types and measurements, 162t
    townhouses out of, 164f

Schloss Lichtenstein (castle), 125f

screens, 12–13, 12f, 13f

sectors, large cities and, 57–58

separation, freestanding communities and, 42

sequential space, 19–20, 20f

service
    fire, 71, 72, 82, 99, 102, 105
    police, 71, 82, 99, 102, 105
    utilities and, 71–72, 175n4

shopping district, 59f

site of social contact, 78–79

site volume ratio (SVR), 32–33, 33f, 153f, 155f. *See
    also* volume ratios

Sitte, Camillo, 31

skyline, 13, 13f, 104f, 177n8. *See also* horizon

skyscrapers, 177n11. *See also* scale

slopes. *See* landforms

slurb, 34, 59, 60

small cities/districts, 56–57

social attributes

child play, 79

economic role, 77

encounter level, 78

function, 76–77

opportunities for relaxation, 79–80

physical, economic, environmental and, 76–80

privacy, 79

safety from crime, 80

site of social contact, 78–79

workforce, 77–78

social contact, site of, 78–79

social scale

event scale and, 16

formal scale and, 15–16

infinite scale and, 16

informal scale and, 15

intimate scale and, 15

software programs, 147, 177n4

soils, three types of, 177n2

Soleri, Paolo, 3, 123, 124, 126f, 127, 128, 176n16, 177n18

Soria y Mata, Arturo, 134

space

articulated, 27

axial, 19, 19f

borrowed, 12, 12f, 95f, 96f, 98f

buildings creating architectural, 10f

defined, enclosed, and enclosing, 26

green, 92

hierarchical, 20, 20f

infinite, 12, 12f

interior, 27

negative, 11–12, 11f, 173n3

positive, 11, 11f, 31, 173n2

sequential, 19–20, 20f

trees creating garden-like, 10f

undifferentiated, 26

spatial quality, 69–70, 174n3

spatial relationships, 70–71

spatial type, 70

special character types

college campus, 110f

industrial areas and, 109–110

maritime heavy industry, 110f

small-scale heavy industry, 110f

sprawl, 40–41, 42f, 43f, 174n11

Standard Industrial Classification System, 174n16

star, 132f, 133

status quo. *See* the blob/sheet

Stein, Clarence, 117

storm-water runoff, 74

streams, 45

structural forms

community and, 112–113

compositional form and, 112

group form and, 112, 113

mega form and, 112, 113

suburb, 34

suburban, 34, 97–99

sub-urban, 34

sub-urban class, 175n17

borrowed open space and undeveloped land, 95f

borrowed open space in cluster development, 96f

commercial with landscaped front yards and, 99f

community character, classes and types and, 91–102

estate and, 99–102

land-treatment systems and, 176n23

lot size and, 175n20

mature urban with sixty-year-old trees, 93f

new suburban with immature trees, 93f

one-acre lot with few twenty-year-old trees, 94f

one-acre wooded lot, 94f

open space ratio and, 175n21

park providing borrowed open space, 96f

suburban, 175n19

suburban and, 97–99

suburban industrial and, 99f

suburban town center with landscaped plaza, 98f

trees arch over street, 95f

trees shelter home, 95f

sub-urban/suburban/suburb/suburbia/slurb, 34

suburbia, 34

Sullivan, Louis, 163

SVR. *See* site volume ratio

symmetry types

asymmetry, 20–21, 21f

symmetry, 20–21, 20f

Tange, Kenzo, 124, 127
Taos Pueblo, 126f
texture, 18, 18f, 173n8
Thiis-Evensen, Thomas, 17
topography, 41f, 42, 119f, 124f
town hall, 126f
towns, 54–55, 54f
the Transect, 3, 120, 173n3
transit suitability, 72
trees, 10f, 14f, 93f, 95f, 155f, 175n9
 as green volume, 93
 lines, 173n14
 as screens, 12f
the Trulli, 119

undifferentiated spaces, 26
undulating landforms, 23
unity, 17
unsymmetrical. *See* asymmetry
Unwin, Raymond, 135
urban, 35, 83–85
urban class
 auto-urban and, 82f, 87–91
 community character, classes and types and, 80–
  91, 175n7
 figure-ground drawing for urban street and, 81f
 street vendor creating activity and, 85f
 urban and, 83–85
 urban core and, 85–87
 urban neighborhood and, 82f
 urban types and, 82–83, 175n8, 175n10
urban core, 35, 82f, 85–87, 85f, 86f
urban types, 82–83, 175n8, 175n10
urban/auto-urban/urban core/urbanization, 35
urbanization, 35
utilities, service and, 71–72, 175n4

valleys, 23f, 24
villages, 49–51, 50f
volume measures, 141
 BVR and, 32, 32f
 LVR and, 32, 32f
 plant unit and, 33, 33f, 34f

SVR and, 32–33, 33f
zoning terms, land use and, 31–33
volume ratios
 community character measurement and, 152–157
 incremental changes in BVR from changes in
  building design, 156t
 large, negative SVR, less desirable, 155f
 mature trees improve SVR and desirability, 155f
 more desirable, lushly landscaped suburban with
  high, positive SVR, 155f
 poorly landscaped new suburb with auto-urban
  character, 154f
 poorly landscaped urban with negative SVR, 155f
 small home, small lot, low BVR, 156f
 two-acre forested estate character, high SVR, 153f
 two-acre lots in open field, suburban character,
  153f
 very large home on small lot, very high BVR
  changes character, 156f
 well-landscaped urban character, 154f

walls, 12, 13, 123f
 edge, gate tower and fortified, 41f
 hedge as, 12f
 river, edges and, 22f
water quality, 74–75
wetlands, 174n15
Weyerhaeuser headquarters building, 127, 128f
workforce, 77–78
Wright, Frank Lloyd, 3

zoning regulations, 120
 agriculture and, 42f, 176n26
 community character measurement and, 177n3
 cookie-cutter zoning and, 28, 175n17
zoning terms, land use and
 designer's lexicon of, 27–33
 figure-ground, 31, 31f
 intensity, 28–30
 land use, 27–28
 LSR, 30–31, 31f
 volume measures, 31–33